T0179351

BUSINESS MODELS

Data Analytics Applications
Series Editor: Jay Liebowitz

PUBLISHED

Big Data in the Arts and Humanities: Theory and Practice
by Giovanni Schiuma and Daniela Carlucci
ISBN 978-1-4987-6585-5

Data Analytics Applications in Education
by Jan Vanthienen and Kristoff De Witte
ISBN: 978-1-4987-6927-3

Data Analytics Applications in Latin America and Emerging Economies
by Eduardo Rodriguez
ISBN: 978-1-4987-6276-2

Data Analytics for Smart Cities
by Amir Alavi and William G. Buttlar
ISBN 978-1-138-30877-0

Data-Driven Law: Data Analytics and the New Legal Services
by Edward J. Walters
ISBN 978-1-4987-6665-4

Intuition, Trust, and Analytics
by Jay Liebowitz, Joanna Paliszkiewicz, and Jerzy Gołuchowski
ISBN: 978-1-138-71912-5

Research Analytics: Boosting University Productivity and Competitiveness through Scientometrics
by Francisco J. Cantú-Ortiz
ISBN: 978-1-4987-6126-0

Sport Business Analytics: Using Data to Increase Revenue and Improve Operational Efficiency
by C. Keith Harrison and Scott Bukstein
ISBN: 978-1-4987-8542-6

BUSINESS MODELS

Innovation, Digital Transformation, and Analytics

Edited by

Iwona Otola and Marlena Grabowska

CRC Press
Taylor & Francis Group
Boca Raton London New York

CRC Press is an imprint of the
Taylor & Francis Group, an **informa** business

AN AUERBACH BOOK

First edition published 2020
by CRC Press
6000 Broken Sound Parkway NW, Suite 300, Boca Raton, FL 33487-2742
and by CRC Press
2 Park Square, Milton Park, Abingdon, Oxon, OX14 4RN

© 2021 Taylor & Francis Group, LLC
CRC Press is an imprint of Taylor & Francis Group, LLC

ISBN: 978-0-367-86279-4 (hbk)
ISBN: 978-1-003-01812-4 (ebk)

Typeset in Caslon
by Cenveo® Publisher Services

Contents

Preface

Iwona Otola, Marlena Grabowska

The concept of business models is constantly growing more important. Its idea has always been present in human business activities. Since the beginning of time, running a business has been forcing the use of logic, according to which it should operate. This logic was called the business model in the management of science literature only in the second half of the 20th century. In recent years, a significantly increased interest in this problem has been observed. The original scientific publications concerned the conceptualization of business models and focused on definitions and the essence of their concept as well as on the identification of their elements. In modern scientific literature, various research trends related to business models may be observed, such as value creation, value chain operationalization, or social and ecological aspects of business models. Also, business model innovation and digital transformation are still important trends.

The purpose of this book is to show how innovation, digital transformation, and composition of value affect the existence and development of business models. To illustrate the background of the discussed topic, the concepts of business models existing in the literature are presented along with their perspective on further development and external conditions that affect them. The above issues were discussed in nine chapters.

Chapter 1 addresses the development of the concept of business models over the years and discusses the essence of innovation in those models with the allowance for the effect of external and internal factors. The authors presented a three-dimensional classification including subject and entity contexts, and the intensity and novelty levels of changes introduced in business models. The main directions of innovative activities, divided into incremental and radical innovation, were discussed.

Chapter 2 refers to digital transformation, which affects the changes in enterprise business models. The authors attempted to evaluate if and how business models are able to analyze digital transformation scenarios. Business model attributes referring to such dimensions as value proposition, value architecture, value network, and value finance, as well as to the attributes on platforms and marketplaces were used for this purpose.

Chapter 3 presents the essence of value composition in business models. Based on the research of high-growth enterprises, factors affecting value in business models were identified. The authors indicated how individual business model elements exert an impact on selected performance measures and which of them are significant for the enterprise value composition, while distinguishing three areas of value creation: value proposition, value creation and delivery system, and value capture.

Chapter 4 is devoted to the diversity of business model aspects in high-growth and high-tech enterprises. The authors distinguished and compared the business model components. The chapter recognizes the specificity of business models in technology-based enterprises. The empirical analysis was conducted based on Estonian high-growth companies from different business fields and technological insensitivity levels.

Chapter 5 presents research on the effect of the environment on the profitability of the high-growth enterprise business models. The chapter incorporates the assumption that conditions resulting from a dynamically changing environment are mostly determined by the place of the company operations. The authors explained the importance of geographical conditions for the business model construction.

The empirical research used multidimensional analysis and on that basis examined the profitability of business models implemented by high-growth enterprises.

Chapter 6 considers issues related to analyzing the employer branding business models. The authors highlighted the differences between generations associated to the perception of jobs and related tasks. The study primarily focused on the characteristics of generation Z as a workforce. In this context, incentives to work and factors affecting the attractiveness of jobs for generation Z were analyzed.

Chapter 7 relates to models of responsible business. It discusses the essence of corporate social responsibility (CSR) concept and characterizes the opportunities and conditions for implementing responsible business models in the enterprise. It presents the social and economic aspects of responsible business models, and also the factors prompting enterprises to make a decision on the implementation of CSR concept in practice.

Chapter 8 presents the analysis of cyber risk, which is a relatively new threat for companies and is associated with the interception of sensitive data, processes, and information. Currently, this type of risk was classified to the sphere of general risk perception by the insurers. The authors of this chapter focused on the analysis and evaluation of cyber risk of customers in insurance companies.

Chapter 9 refers to decision algorithms and their importance in business analytics. Open data resources in public space provide information for creating algorithms. The authors discussed techniques of data analysis, which affect the decision-making and the implementation of adequate analytical tools. Based on open data, the authors used selected analytical tools to assess three different cases, that is, the prediction of the sports competition results, the prediction of the cold sickness, and the enterprise cyber risk assessment.

Theoretical consideration was based on a critical review of the latest world literature and was supported by empirical research. In empirical research on business models, primary and secondary data were used, based on which the inference process was carried out using quantitative and qualitative methods. These studies were conducted using such methods as exploratory research, case studies, questionnaire surveys, interviews, the methods of multidimensional statistical analysis, neural networks, regression analysis, and others.

This book is a compendium of knowledge about the use of business models in the context of innovative activities, digital transformation, and value composition. The creation of this book was intended to combine the theory and practice regarding the above issues in the international perspective. The book offers a look at business models currently used in companies (especially high-growth enterprises) in various countries of the world and indicates the prospects for their development, as well as possible global, external threats.

We hope this book will be an interesting reading for the researches, specialists, and people involved in business.

Editors' Biographies

Iwona Otola is an associate professor of the Faculty of Management, Czestochowa University of Technology, Poland. Her scientific interests focus on strategic management, resource-based view, business models, entrepreneurship, and competitiveness of the enterprises. She is an author of numerous scientific publications, articles, and chapters in books and textbooks. In 2002, she was on a scholarship at the Central European University (Hungary), where she was a participant in the program Intergovernmental Fiscal Relations and Local Financial Management in association with World Bank Institute and Local Government and Public Service Reform Initiative of the Open Society Institute, Budapest, Hungary. Since 2000, she has been a member of many research teams implementing projects for the Częstochowa University of Technology and companies from the energy sector. She has extensive experience in organizational activities, co-organized conferences, and international scientific workshops. Since 2015, Professor Otola has been actively cooperating with Centro Estadual de Educação Tecnológica Paula Souza in Brazil. She is a member of Polish Economic Society since 2015 and the Committee of Organization and Management of the Polish Academy of Sciences since 2017.

Marlena Grabowska is an associate professor of the Faculty of Management, Czestochowa University of Technology, Poland. Her research focuses on management issues, such as business models, competitiveness and innovativeness of enterprises, enterprise value management, and corporate governance. She has published over 130 scientific publications, that is, articles, chapters in books and text-books. In 2005, she received a supervisor's grant from the Minister of Science and Information Society Technologies related to the implementation of her doctoral thesis, "Analysis of the resource management strategy of the enterprise." Professor Grabowska has extensive experience in organizational activities in higher education. She was a co-organizer of conferences and scientific workshops, as well as the Austrian-Polish Economic Forums. In the years 2009–2010, she also worked as an expert on monitoring and financial accounting for the UE projects. In 2008 and 2009, Marlena Grabowska participated in scientific seminars in Vlotho, Germany, organized by the Polish Economic Society and Ludwig-Erhard-Stiftung, sacrificed to social problems of market economy and European integration. She is a member of the Committee of Organization and Management of the Polish Academy of Sciences since 2017 and Polish Economic Society since 2008. She is the vice-president of the Polish-Austrian Society – Częstochowa Branch.

Contributors' Biographies

Andreas Ahrens is a professor for Signal and System Theory at the Hochschule Wismar, University of Technology, Business and Design, Germany. He is the co-author of numerous scientific publications, articles, and chapters in books and textbooks. His main field of interest includes error-correcting codes, multiple-input multiple-output systems, iterative detection for both wireline and wireless communication, as well as social computing.

David Nicolas Bartolini is a PhD student at the Universidad Politécnica de Madrid, Spain and principal cyber security consultant. He practices scientific research, and he is an experienced security practitioner with over five years' experience in the field, and his certifications include CISSP and CISM. He is currently an information security officer at a large enterprise. He is the author of scientific publications, articles, and chapters in books on the usage of Cyber Risk Analysis. His research interests include issues of machine learning and decision management, in relation to IT Security.

César Benavente-Peces is an assistant professor in the Department of Audio-Visual Engineering and Communications at the Faculty ETS Ingeniería y Sistemas de Telecomunicación of the Universidad

Politécnica de Madrid (UPM), Spain. Additionally, he is with the Radio Engineering Research Group (GIRA) which is part of the Centro de Electrónica Industrial (CEI) of the UPM. He is the author of numerous scientific contributions including international journal, conferences, and book chapters in the field of information and communication technologies (ICTs). He is/has been the leader of many research projects funded by the European Union, national and regional governments, and has contracts with the industry. His research interests include wireless communications, Internet of Things (IoT), sensor networks, mobile networks, education innovation, and ICT applications in the industry and management. He is/has been the conference chair of international conferences, guest editor of some international relevant journals.

Ágnes Csiszárik-Kocsir, PhD, is an associate professor and director of Business and Management Institute at the Karoly Keleti Faculty of Business and Management at the Obuda University in Hungary. Her main teaching and research areas are project investment, corporate finance, and project management.

Mónika Garai-Fodor, PhD, is an associate professor and vice-dean for Education at the Karoly Keleti Faculty of Business and Management at the Obuda University in Hungary. Her main teaching and research areas are consumer behavior, marketing research, and marketing communication.

Patricia K. Inoue has a Professional Master's degree in Productive Systems, Centro Estadual de Educação Tecnológica Paula Souza in Brazil and she acts as a consultant in Business Transformation focusing on strategic development for companies in various segments. She participates in research groups in the areas of digital transformation, business models, processes, and start-up ecosystem with production of scientific publications, articles, and book chapters. Interested in research in the areas of productive systems, innovation, and new systemic and process implementations in various business environments.

Merike Kaseorg is an assistant of entrepreneurship at the Faculty of Economics and Business Administration of the University of Tartu, Estonia. She practices scientific research as well as teaching and is the author of numerous scientific publications, articles, and textbooks. She has developed specialized courses on Introduction to Entrepreneurship and Basics of Business Information Processing, and also teaches courses on Principles of Entrepreneurship, Business Plan and Entrepreneurship in Dentistry. Her field of research is entrepreneurial university, entrepreneurship education and training, social entrepreneurship, family firms, and small business.

Agata Mesjasz-Lech, PhD, is an associate professor and vice-dean of the Faculty of Management, Czestochowa University of Technology, Poland. She defended the doctoral thesis with distinction at the Faculty of Management of the Częstochowa University of Technology in 2004. She held her habilitation in economics from Czestochowa University of Technology in 2012. Since 2008, Agata Mesjasz-Lech has been a member of the Polish Economic Society (Branch in Częstochowa) and since 2011, a member of the European Association of Environmental and Natural Resources Economists. Agata Mesjasz-Lech has scientific interests concentrated on the issues of logistics and management, and in particular, on the application of quantitative methods in logistics processes. She is the author of more than 100 publications. She presented her conclusions during conferences organized in Poland and abroad.

Natalia Myronova is an assistant professor in the Software Engineering Department at the Computer Sciences and Technology Faculty of the Zaporizhzhia Polytechnic National University, Ukraine. She conducts scientific research, as well as teaching. She is the author of numerous scientific publications, articles, and papers on the usage of information technology in group decision-making and machine vision. Her interests include issues of recognition of music and video images, also design and development of information systems for detection and tracking of objects in static frames or video streams. Since 2013, she has been the coach of student teams for International Collegiate Programming Contest (ICPC) and coordinator of the first and second stages of ICPC.

Marcelo T. Okano is an associate professor in the Professional Master's Program in Productive Systems at the Post-graduation, Extension and Research Unit of the State Center of Technological Education Paula Souza (CEETEPS) in Brazil. He practices scientific research, as well as teaching. He is the author of numerous scientific publications, articles, chapters in books and textbooks on the ICT, and Management and Production Engineering. His research interests include issues of Digital Transformation and Business Models.

Marcin Ratajczak, PhD, is an associate professor in the Warsaw University of Life Sciences, Poland. He obtained a PhD in economics in 2009 defending his dissertation on the activity and economic situation of small- and medium-sized enterprises from rural areas. In 2019, he obtained the degree of habilitated doctor of social sciences in the discipline of management and quality science. Participates in conducting educational classes in the field of work psychology, entrepreneurship, and elements of human resource management. Scientific and research activity focuses on issues of small- and medium-sized entrepreneurship and CSR. He is the author of many scientific publications in domestic and foreign magazines, as well as the author of two monographs on responsible business on the example of agribusiness companies. He has been awarded many times at conferences for the best articles and the best presentations in terms of substance. He participated in international internships from the Atlantis Youth Exchange program in Norway and international conferences, including in Hungary, Slovakia, and Ukraine. He was the laureate of the "Mazowiecki Doctoral Scholarship" awarded by the Marshal of the Mazowieckie Voivodeship and received several times the Rector's Award for scientific and publishing achievements.

Mervi Raudsaar is an associate professor of entrepreneurship at the School of Economics and Business Administration and an associate professor of social entrepreneurship at Viljandi Culture Academy, University of Tartu, Estonia. She teaches and researches entrepreneurship and has also developed special courses on social entrepreneurship, creative industries, and entrepreneurship for educational studies. She is a member of the research team of Nordic NoE: Social Entrepreneurship Network. She is also a member of EMPOWER-SE (Empowering the next generation of social enterprise scholars) network. She has worked as an expert for Analysis of Social Enterprise Support System (2017) and other local and -international institutions (eg, OECD, European Commission). The research interests of her include issues of entrepreneurship education and training, entrepreneurial university, entrepreneurship, business models, and entrepreneurial ecosystem.

Rosinei Batista Ribeiro is an associate professor in the Centro Paula Souza and UNIFATEA, Brazil. He practices scientific research, as well as teaching. He is the author of numerous scientific publications, articles, chapters in books and textbooks in the areas of Industrial Design, Materials Engineering and Production, focusing on Design and Materials, Product Design, Social Technologies, Experiment Planning (DOE), Manufacturing Processes, Corrosion, Materialography, and Supply Chain Management (SCM). The research interests of him include design, innovation, material, and production. He holds a PhD degree in Mechanical Engineering and Postdoctorate in Mechanical Engineering at the Paulista State University.

Eliane A. Simões is an associate professor in the Professional Master's Program in Productive Systems at the Post-graduation, extension and research Unit of the State Centre of Technological Education Paula Souza (CEETEPS), Brazil. She is the author of numerous scientific publications, articles, chapters in books and textbooks on the innovation, management, and business models.

Marek Szajt, PhD, is an associate professor of the Częstochowa University of Technology and head of Department of Econometrics and Statistics of Faculty of Management, Poland. His research interests relate, in particular, the study of innovation in the micro-, meso-, and macro scale, spatial research, simulation analysis, econometric modelling using spatio-temporal sample. He is the author and co-author of over 100 scientific publications, and reports carried out on behalf of local government institutions and enterprises.

Katarzyna Szymczyk, PhD, is an assistant professor at the Faculty of Management, Czestochowa University of Technology, Poland. She is an academic teacher and a researcher. Her scientific interests concentrate on the strategic management, economics, corporate finance, sustainable development in management and international aspects of entrepreneurship, as well as on the concept of industry 4.0 and the circular economy in relation to strategic management and company value building.

Galyna Tabunshchyk is a professor in the Software Engineering Department at the Computer Sciences and Technology Faculty of the Zaporizhzhia Polytechnic National University, Ukraine. She defended PhD in 2001 in Control Systems and Processes. She is the author of numerous scientific publications, articles, chapters in books, one monography, and five textbooks. She is the leader of scientific group in Reliability of informational systems and leader researcher of the funded scientific projects in the field of verification of informational systems. Under her supervision, there were defended two PhD works in the field of Informational Technologies. She is university coordinator of the Erasmus+ KA1 and Erasmus+ KA2 projects. Her research interests are Software Engineering, Verification of Informational Systems, Data Analytics, and Decision-making systems.

Piia Vettik-Leemet is a junior research fellow of entrepreneurship at the Faculty of Economics and Business Administration of the University of Tartu, Estonia. She practices scientific research as well as teaching the courses on Principles of Entrepreneurship and has developed a special course on Growing Company and Management. She has worked as a business consultant for 11 years and has more than 5 years of experience as a business development manager at Tartu Biotechnology Park and BioMed Incubator. She has helped to develop numerous business models for high-growth and high-tech start-ups. She also participated in the management team of Baltics biggest business festival sTARTUp Day. The research interests of her include issues of innovation, entrepreneurship, business models, start-ups, and innovation paradoxes.

Aneta Włodarczyk, PhD, is an assistant professor at the Faculty of Management, Czestochowa University of Technology, Poland. She earned her MA degree in mathematics from Jagiellonian University and PhD in management science form Czestochowa University of Technology. She is a member of the Eurasia Business and Economics Society and Scientific Society of Organization and Management (Branch in Czestochowa). She has conducted extensive research and written widely on topics related to the energy industry and its impact on the environment, the influence of the EU ETS on corporate value, carbon risk management, sustainable development, the Environmental Kuznets Curve Hypothesis, and econometric modelling in the presence of structural breaks.

Acknowledgments

"Coming together is a beginning,
staying together is progress,
and working together is success."

Henry Ford

Cooperation produces fine results through common discussions and conversations. It makes possible to strengthen relations and leads to success in completing projects that seem impossible at the start.

We sincerely thank our contributor authors, without whom this book would never have been created. We express a deep sense of gratitude for their commitment and creative work on individual chapters.

We would like to thank the reviewers for their comments that contributed to the final shape of the book. We also express our gratitude to all those who were engaged in the creation of this book and believed that creation was possible.

We would like to thank Jay Liebowitz and John Wyzalek at Taylor & Francis Group for supporting us in this project.

Iwona Otola
Marlena Grabowska

1

Innovation in Business Models

MARLENA GRABOWSKA, IWONA OTOLA, AND KATARZYNA SZYMCZYK

Contents

1.1 Introduction

Modern organizations are being put under pressure related to maintaining the competitive advantage in the ever-changing environment. The heterogeneous economic conditions for enterprises' operation often impose the need for innovative solutions in various areas of their activity. Jensen and Sund (2017) suggest that awareness of the need to find new solutions in a business model is usually initiated by changes perceived in the external environment, such as changes in customer expectations. Enterprises continuously look for new operation methods, which could improve their competitive position. An effective way of confronting environmental challenges is the implementation of innovation into a business model (Fjeldstad and Snow, 2018). Innovative solutions may be introduced in the product, process, or organization areas. The system of connections and cause-effect relations established between individual elements of a business model should be flexible enough to accept modifications and support innovation. A new solution implemented in a business model not always equals the achievement of market success. Nevertheless, enterprises decide to introduce innovation related to their business model in order to maintain the value generated at the previous level or to try to increase this value creation level.

The purpose of this chapter is to discuss, based on literature studies, the concept of innovative solutions in business models. The theoretical nature of this analysis imposes two significant diagnostic requirements related to the problem research procedure. The first is the necessity of introducing theoretical foundation for the importance of innovation in business models being discussed, and the second is the identification of key directions of innovative activities. The basis for achieving such purpose is the analysis of the business model interpretation and its features that allows to discover the conceptual assumptions for the business model as well as innovative activities implemented in it.

1.2 Development of the Business Model Concept

The problem of business models has been becoming more important recently, both in theoretical and practical context. It is the subject of numerous scientific and popular science publications, the issue addressed and discussed at scientific conferences, and also the essence of business meetings and the subject of discourse at meetings of various management bodies. In scientific terms, the source of this concept should be identified with the 1957 publication of Bellman et al. on multiplayer business games. However, only in the late 1990s the issue of business models became broadly discussed and cited in the subject literature. Sorrentino and Smarra (2015) indicate that it is a direct consequence of three different factors: the advent of the Internet, rapid growth in emerging markets, and the development of the industry and organizations dependent on post-industrial technologies.

The growth of the business model topic is also related to its multi-criteria concept and the emphasis on its various aspects. The following overview of selected definitions of the business model idea allows to extract the key concepts that reflect the basic approach to this problem as well as the development of its perception in the subject literature.

One example of the early attempts to interpret the business model concept can be the publication by Boulton et al. (1997), who emphasize this is a unique combination of tangible and intangible assets, providing an organization with the ability to create value. Timmers (1998) defined the business model as an architecture for products, services, and information streams, containing a description of various business activities and their roles. The author also stated that it is a description of benefits for various business entities and also of revenue sources. On the other hand, Venkatraman and Henderson (1998) indicated that the structure of a business model is created through the harmony of three vectors (i.e., customer interaction, acquiring resources, and expanding knowledge) and a strong IT platform.

Some approaches may be distinguished from the later studies on the business model that define it as a concept consisting of numerous related elements. Amit and Zott (2001) indicated the business model as describing a transaction element's design, structure, and management in a way that allows for value creation based on the use of emerging business opportunities. Hamel (2000) identifies the business model concept as customer relations, compositions of key strategies, strategic resources, and value networks. Magretta (2002) investigates this issue from a more general perspective and states that business models are stories explaining how a company operates. The author also claims that a good business model should answer the following questions: Who is the customer? What is the value for the customer? How do we make money in this business? What is the underlying economic logic that explains how we can deliver value to customers at an appropriate cost?

Definitions of the business model often point various factors characterizing this problem out. However, scientific studies reveal leading and often similar categories emphasizing the essence of the business model. Wagner et al. (2015), in this context, note that approaches interpreting the business model may demonstrate similar elements describing this issue.

In many approaches, the business model is being related to the "dominant logic" concept. Prahalad and Bettis (1986) understood this term as a set of norms and principles that should be followed by managers in order to organize a company operation properly as well as try to pursue and use emerging market opportunities. This approach emphasizes the rationality feature in the company functioning. Osterwalder and Pigneur (2002) wrote in this context that it is natural that every owner and manager is familiar with the principles of their company operations and the logic behind its value creation, meaning that they understand the business model of the company. Many definitions of business models include references to company operation logic. Shafer et al. (2005) indicate that the business model base refers to the logic determining the creation and maintenance of value. This concept is defined in a similar context by Linder and Cantrell (2000), who claim that in brief approach the business model may be described as a basic logic guiding organizations that create value. On the other hand, Chesbrough and Rosenbloom (2002) indicated that the business model is a heuristic logic combining the potential of technology with the outcome of economic value.

Further, interpretations of the "business model" concept introduced above illustrate that its essence is also largely associated with the category of value. The concept of value is one of the basic components of those definitions. However, researches in this field highlight various aspects of value. Osterwalder and Pigneur (2010) indicated that a business model identifies how a given organization creates, provides, and captures value. When referring value to the entity to which it is attributed, the business model definitions also mention direct beneficiaries of value, that is, customers as well as enterprises acquiring value. In this context, Teece (2010) states that a business model is a description of the logic, the data, and other elements that are the basis for value offered to customers, as well as a clear distribution of revenues and costs for enterprises that deliver the value. The subject literature reveals a similar interpretation defining the business model as a method of running the business, expressed by determining how an enterprise produces value, by establishing the place of a given enterprise among its partners in the value chain, and by identifying a form of cooperation with customers who generate revenues (Rappa, 2004). Therefore, the value generated according to the business model construction serves the enhancement of customer relations and thus contributes to the stronger competitive position of the enterprise.

The business model interpretations presented above emphasize its significant role in value creation. In theoretical approach, value is a dominant dimension of a business model. When drawing conclusions from the semantic analysis of the business model concept, it may be indicated that its proper construction and effective implementation into the enterprise favor value creation. Thus, in the context of ensuring the enterprise's ability to generate value, it becomes crucial to be able to introduce changes and innovative solutions in a business model.

1.3 Essence of Innovative Activities in the Business Model

Modern turbulent economic conditions keep making it necessary to introduce innovation into various areas and spheres of activity. In order to effectively respond to ever-changing market requirements, enterprises have to improve currently manufactured products and work on creating completely new products or technological solutions. Therefore, an organization's operation is immanently associated with the innovation concept, which should also refer to enterprise activities logic, thus affecting the verification of a business model and adapt it to market conditions. It should be emphasized that the useful life of a business model is limited, and it becomes necessary to introduce innovation into the model.

The literature on the subject indicates that innovation in business models is a change in the enterprise business logic (Teece, 2010). Innovation in business models is also interpreted as changes introduced in the area of creating, delivering, and capturing mechanisms that encourage customers to pay for value (Baden-Fuller and Morgan, 2010; Teece, 2010). On the other hand, Johnson et al. (2008) perceive business model innovation as a very strong means of management that helps companies in their struggle with modern global market conditions of competition and dynamic changes. Thus, it has been highlighted that practitioners from a wide variety of industries actively seek guidance on how to innovate their business models in order to improve their ability to both create and capture value (Casadesus-Masanell and Ricart, 2010).

It should be noticed that innovation in business models may refer both to enterprises already operating on the market and holding an established position and to entities creating new business models in the form of a start-up. Much smaller part of the literature focuses on incumbent companies that already have established business models, and their decisions to add new business models that can be disruptive (Bogers et al., 2015; Kim and Min, 2015; Sosna et al., 2010).

Enterprises operating on the market look for new business models that can be added to the models already existing in the enterprise, or can replace some existing model with a new solution. The literature on business models indicates that developing new business models in particular (as opposed to simpler incremental product improvements) poses a challenge for innovative entities (Friis-Holm Egfjord and Sund, 2020). The existing cognitive barriers may result in the introduction of incorrect solutions in implemented innovative activities, as innovative directions of business models depend on the interpretation and perception of external factors affecting the companies. Friis-Holm Egfjord and Sund (2020) prove that such perceptual differences can help to explain one of the open questions of innovation management: Why do so many incumbents appear to fail at radical business model innovation? The reason for the failure of innovation in business models may originate from the differences in perception which changes in the environment are the most significant. The diversity of perception of change needs in business models may lead to the assumption of incorrect solutions and failed innovative activities. Hence, the introduction of changes is associated with the risk of mismatching the business model with market requirements that may result in losing customer relations or the part of the market segment. Therefore, it is crucial to determine the way of exercising such actions in business models implemented that allow to achieve market success. It is very important to expertly recognize those changes in the environment, in particular, including customer expectations.

However, McDonald et al. (2019) notice that environmental factors are not only an impulse for innovation in business models. The company management can proactively develop or adapt a business model (Martins et al., 2015). In this case, the reasons for innovative activities are external factors that constrict value generation in the business model. Changes within the organization are also affected by internal stimulants that become determinants of business model development. Reinhold et al. (2011) in such a case distinguish the following factors: organizational culture, available knowledge and skills, diversified resources, and employee skills. Zentes et al. (2013) also indicate that the surplus of organizational resources and competences is a major incentive for the introduction of changes in the existing business model. Therefore, there is a need for management intervention in order to increase the flexibility of the organization. In this situation, it becomes essential to alert internal stakeholders and draw their attention to the factors because of which an existing business model may have worked in the past but is no longer viable. Knowing the elements that have to be changed and when to change them is thus a key component of the business model management.

1.4 Typology of Innovative Activities in Business Models

Innovation in business models can be considered using various typologies. Schallmo (2013) proposes a three-dimensional classification that allows for a subject context (relating to the business model elements), entity context (including the reference unit), and the intensity level of changes introduced.

According to the subject criterion, changes in a business model relate to its elements. Such an approach requires first the identification of components based on one of the concepts referring to the business model architecture. It should be emphasized that the literature presents various proposals for determining this structure, which often illustrate large discrepancies between the concepts of particular researchers of this subject. They show different areas of the business model optics and indicate their generalized or detailed nature (more on this subject see Chapter 3). Hence, innovative activities implemented in the area of different elements are of ununiform nature. Ununiform level of interference in the model overall structure, in this case, means a change in a single component, in greater number of components, or in all components of the business model.

Grabowska (2015) notices that subject changes are implemented considering specific business model stakeholders. In general terms, the basic recipient of business model changes, and the subjects verifying these changes are customers, who respond adequately to the changed value proposition. Nevertheless, some other value recipients are indicated that respond to changes in the business model of a given company. These include competitors from the sector where the company operates, or key business partners.

The level of intensity or novelty of the business model changes may take various formats related to the scope of interference in a given model. Bieger and Reinhold (2011), given these formats, distinguish three basic patterns of a company development, resulting from the business model transformations. These changes can take the form of quantitative growth, incremental innovation, and radical innovation.

The quantitative growth refers to the increase in the number of transactions or the frequency of transactions with existing customers. In this case, there are no innovative activities, thus quantitative changes do not cause a transformation in the business model architecture (Grabowska and Otola, 2016). Creation of new value uses the existing model. It remains unchanged, but is extended. Calling it an innovative business model is inappropriate in this case.

On the other hand, incremental and radical activities are innovative activities and contribute to changes in the business model. In the case of incremental innovation, base components of the business model are smoothly modified, or mutual relations between its elements are evolutionary modified. Incremental innovation is an innovation of low novelty level, which usually translates into lower risk and lower costs, but also has lower effect on the financial result (Damanpour, 1996; Martínez-Ros and Orfila-Sintes, 2009; Souto, 2015). Incremental changes are gradual and do not interfere deeply in the architecture of the business model. This remains in accordance with the overall characteristics of incremental innovation, which refer to relatively small adaptations of existing products, that is, only small changes in technology, design, product restart, and the line extension, adding an attribute to existing service (Lennerts et al., 2019; Souto, 2015).

The radical approach to innovation in business models is associated with the process of creative destruction proposed by Schumpeter (1942), which involves a constant internal revolutionization of existing technologies and production methods, continuous destruction of the old ones and creation of the new, more effective ones. Such an approach to innovation indicates their high novelty level and thus incorporates high risk and also great opportunities and challenges. When relating radical innovation to the business model, it should be stated that it causes fundamental transformations in the model elements or construction. Hence, innovative activities are of an intense nature. Zentes et al. (2013) emphasize that overall radical changes in the business model usually include focusing on new markets, new customer segments, but also relate to the company response to new challenges and customer needs, aimed at providing them with innovative value. In addition, radical transformations of the business model may affect the competitiveness of the industry, resulting in the alteration of its existing principles of market conduct.

1.5 Conclusion

The considerations resulting from the literature studies illustrate the variety of definition approaches to the business model concept. Currently, business models become a noticeable subject of scientific discourse. Studies on this subject may be considered with the distinction of a broader (detailed) and narrower (general) attempts to explain this issue. The management science literature highlights the importance of business models in shaping competitive position and establishing competitive advantage. A number of considerations on business models focus on generating, delivering, and capturing value. It has been noticed that business models, being the login of companies' operations, describe how these companies build value. In this situation, it is important to ensure the ability of business models to compose value through their development and implementation of innovative solutions.

Ever-changing competitive environment makes enterprises introduce activities adapting them to new conditions. The impulse to introduce changes in company operation is one of the factors that originate inside the enterprise. Business models become an important area of innovative activities being introduced. The implementation of innovative solutions in business models of a given company increases its toughness in the competitive market.

In addition, theoretical considerations indicate that innovation in business models can take various forms. In general, they are being implemented in relation to the business model elements, reference units (stakeholders), or with regard to the level of intensity and novelty of changes introduced. In the latter case, changes in the business model take the form of quantitative growth, incremental innovation, and radical innovation. It should be emphasized that the scope of innovative activities in the business model depends on the current needs of a given enterprise. The proper recognition of these needs is therefore a crucial factor of success in value composition.

References

Amit, R., Zott, C. (2001). Value creation in e-business. *Strategic Management Journal, 22*, pp. 493–520.

Baden-Fuller, C., Morgan, M.S. (2010). Business models as models. *Long Range Planning, 43 (2–3)*, pp. 156–171.

Bellman, R., Clark, C.E., Malcom, D.G., Craft, C.J., Ricciardi, F.M. (1957). On the construction of a multi-stage, multi-person business game. *Operations Research, 5(4)*, pp. 469–503.

Bieger, T., Reinhold, S. (2011). Das wertbasierte Geschäftsmodell – ein aktualisierter Strukturierungsansatz. In: T. Bieger, D. zu Knyphausen-Aufsess, C. Krys (eds.), *Innovative Geschäftsmodelle – Konzeptionelle Grundlagen, Gestaltungsfelder und unternehmerische Praxis*. Berlin-Heideberg: Springer-Verlag, pp. 13–70.

Bogers, M., Sund, K.J., Villarroel, J.A. (2015). The organizational dimension of business model exploration: Evidence from the European postal industry. In: N.J. Foss, T. Saebi, (eds.), *Business model innovation: The organizational dimension*. Oxford, UK: University Press, pp. 269–288.

Boulton, R.E.S., Libert, B.D., Samek, S.M. (1997). *Cracking the value code: How successful businesses are creating wealth in the new economy*. New York: Harper Collins Publishers.

Casadesus-Masanell, R., Ricart, J.E. (2010). From strategy to business models and onto tactics. *Long Range Planning, 43(2–3)*, pp. 195–215.

Chesbrough, H., Rosenbloom, R.S. (2002). The role of the business model in capturing value from innovation: Evidence from Xerox Corporation's technology spin-off companies. *Industrial and Corporate Change, 11*, pp. 529–555.

Damanpour, F. (1996). Organizational complexity and innovation: Developing and testing multiple contingency models. *Management Science, 42(5)*, pp. 693–716.

Fjeldstad, Ø., Snow, C.C. (2018). Business models and organization design. *Long Range Planning, 51(1)*, pp. 32–39.

Friis-Holm Egfjord, K., Sund, K.J. (2020). Do you see what I see? How differing perceptions of the environment can hinder radical business model innovation. *Technological Forecasting & Social Change, 150(119787)*, pp. 1–10.

Grabowska M., Otola, I. (2016). Zmiany w modelach biznesu w przedsiębiorstwach inteligentnych. In: S. Gregorczyk, W. Mierzejewska (eds.), *Zarządzanie przedsiębiorstwem inteligentnym. Wybrane zagadnienia*. Warszawa: SGH, pp. 85–96.

Grabowska, M. (2015). Concepts and perspectives of business model development. *Przegląd Organizacji, Nr 12(911)*, pp. 65–72.

Hamel, G. (2000). *Leading the revolution*. Boston: Harvard Business School Press.

Jensen, H., Sund, K.J. (2017). The journey of business model innovation in media agencies: Towards a three-stage process model. *Journal of Media Business Studies, 14(4)*, pp. 282–298.

Johnson, M.W., Christensen, C.M., Kagermann, H. (2008). Reinventing your business model. *Harvard Business Review, 87* (December 12), pp. 51–59.

Kim, S.K., Min, S. (2015). Business model innovation performance: When does adding a new business model benefit an incumbent? *Strategic Entrepreneurship Journal, 9(1)*, pp. 34–57.

Lennerts, S., Schulze, A., Tomczak, T. (2020). The asymmetric effects of exploitation and exploration on radical and incremental innovation performance: An uneven affair. *European Management Journal, 38(1)*, pp. 121–134. Doi.org/10.1016/j.emj.2019.06.002.

Linder, J.C., Cantrell, S. (2000). *Changing Business models: surveying the landscape.* A Working Paper from the Accenture Institute for Strategic Change.

Magretta, J. (2002). Why business models matter? *Harvard Business Review, 80(5)*, pp. 86–92.

Martínez-Ros, E., Orfila-Sintes, F. (2009). Innovation activity in the hotel industry. *Technovation, 29*, pp. 632–641.

Martins, L.L., Rindova, V.P., Greenbaum, B.E. (2015). Unlocking the hidden value of concepts: A cognitive approach to BMI. *Strategic Entrepreneurship Journal, 9*, pp. 99–117.

McDonald, R.E., Masselli, J.J., Chanda, B. (2019). Nonprofit business model innovation as a response to existential environmental threats: Performing arts in the United States. *Journal of Business Research.* Doi.org/10.1016/j.jbusres.2019.12.022.

Osterwalder, A., Pigneur, Y. (2002). *An eBusiness model ontology for modeling eBusiness.* 15th Bled Electronic Commerce Conference e-Reality: Constructing the e-Economy. Bled, Slovenia.

Osterwalder, A., Pigneur, Y. (2010). *Business model generation: A handbook for visionaries, game changers, and challengers.* Hoboken: John Wiley & Sons.

Prahalad, C., Bettis, R. (1986). The dominant logic: The new linkage between diversity and performance. *Strategic Management Journal, 7*, pp. 485–501.

Rappa, M. (2004). The utility business model and the future of computing services. *IBM Systems Journal, 43(1)*, pp. 32–42

Reinhold, S., Reuter, E., Bieger T. (2011). Innovative Geschäftsmodelle – die Sicht des Managements. In: T. Bieger, D. zu Knyphausen-Aufsess, C. Krys (eds.), *Innovative Geschäftsmodelle –Konzeptionelle Grundlagen, Gestaltungsfelder und unternehmerische Praxis.* Berlin-Heidelberg: Springer-Verlag, pp. 71–91.

Schallmo, D. (2013). *Geschäftsmodell-Innovation. Grundlage, bestehende Ansätze, methodisches Vorgehen und B2B-Geschäftsmodelle.* Wiesbaden: Springer-Verlag.

Schumpeter, J. (1942). *Capitalism, socialism and democracy.* New York: Harper & Brothers.

Shafer, S.M., Smith, H.J., Linder, J.C. (2005). The power of business models. *Business Horizons, 48*, pp. 199–207.

Sorrentino, M., Smarra, M. (2015). The term "Business Model" in financial reporting: Does it need a proper definition? *Open Journal of Accounting, 4*, pp. 11–22

Sosna, M., Trevinyo-Rodríguez, R.N., Velamuri, S.R. (2010). Business model innovation through trial-and-error learning: The Naturhouse case. *Long Range Planning, 43(2)*, pp. 383–407.

Souto, J.E. (2015). Business model innovation and business concept innovation as the context of incremental innovation and radical innovation. *Tourism Management, 51*, pp. 142–155.

Teece, D.J. (2010). Business models, business strategy and innovation. *Long Range Planning, 43*, pp. 172–194.

Timmers, P. (1998). Business models for electronic markets. *Electronic Markets, 8*, pp. 3–8.

Venkatraman, N., Henderson, J.C. (1998). Real strategies for virtual organizing. *Sloan Management Review, 40(1)*, pp. 33–48.

Wagner, T., Tilly, R., Bodenbenner, Ph., Seltitz, A., Schoder, D. (2015). Geschäftsmodellinnovation in der Praxis: Ergebnisse einer Expertenbefragung zu Business model Canvas und Co. In: O. Thomas, F. Teuteberg (eds.), *Proceedings der 12. Internationalen Tagung Wirtschaftsinformatik (WI 2015)*. Osnabrück, pp. 1298–1312.

Zentes, J., Steinhauer, R., Lonnes, V. (2013). *Geschäftsmodell-Evolution: Unternehmensentwicklung als Dynamisierung von Kernkompetenzen.* Frankfurt am Main: Institut für Handel & Internationales Marketing (H.I.MA.) der Universität des Saarlandes.

2

Business Models in the Digital Transformation Era

MARCELO T. OKANO,
PATRICIA K. INOUE,
ELIANE A. SIMÕES, AND
ROSINEI BATISTA RIBEIRO

Contents

2.1 Introduction

Companies that are adapting to new technologies and becoming digitalized, structured in new ways, are called digital organizations of the future. According to Chew (2015), they are called DOOTF (digital organizations of the future).

Digital transformation is profoundly changing how value is captured and created, the new companies with new and innovative business models are born, and existing companies must rethink their business models to become digital (Itälä, 2015).

Digital transformation of a business means discussing various types of business transformation by introducing or adapting value-added services and using new technologies to generate a direct impact on the delivery of results and the customer experience, making it one of the company's main guidelines. Channels and processes will also be transformed, and the need to look for new models and revenue streams based on customer requirements will become necessary and, consequently, it will be mandatory to change the company's internal culture to include "digital" at the heart of everything that is being done (Llorente, 2016).

In more digitally mature companies, the ability to adapt or redesign the business is determined in large part by a digital strategy clearly supported by leaders who foster a culture capable of changing and inventing the new. In digital transformation, one of the most evident attitudes is the taking of risks as a cultural norm, causing the most advanced companies to seek new levels of competitive advantage. Another equally important aspect is the preparation to adapt to the challenges and functioning of the company, thinking about the retention and attraction of new talents as employees of all ages that seek compatible opportunities to work and develop in companies committed to digital progress (Kane et al., 2015).

In view of this process evidenced in the academic and business literature, the contributions are (a) to verify in which factors companies should focus on the digital transformation of their business, through bibliographic review and interviews with expert consultants in this area; and (b) to demonstrate how business models can analyze the scenarios of digital transformation through business models.

2.2 Theoretical Framework

2.2.1 Digital Companies

For Swanton and Lehong (2017), digital business is a creation of new business designs that blend the physical and digital worlds. This creates an unprecedented convergence of people, businesses, and things that change business models and create new revenue opportunities.

Turban et al. (2015) define a digital business as a company that uses digital technologies and networks in the activities of buying and selling products and services, customer service, collaboration with business partners, conducting communications and transactions within the organization.

For Burton et al. (2018), a digital business or enterprise is a business that exploits data and analysis. While data also exists in analog business, in digital it becomes foggy, riskier, and more valuable; and analytics underpin the new intelligent and improved mode of business. Even if the organization has not yet decided to adopt a digital business platform, data and analytics need to be explored to improve business results and put data and analytics at the center of the strategy.

In the digital age, connection economics describes value creation by increasing the density of interactions between companies, people, and things. This new connection economy will continue to accelerate, change the way companies invest in new products, physical assets, information technologies, and people.

For Dörner and Edelman (2015), becoming digital in some cases requires being open to reexamining your whole way of doing business and understanding where the new frontiers of value lie. For some companies, understanding these new frontiers may consist of developing entirely new businesses in adjacent categories, while for others it may mean identifying and pursuing new value groups in existing industries. In addition, going digital means being in tune with how customer decision-making is evolving in the broadest sense. Understanding how customer behaviors and expectations are developing inside and outside of your business and industry is crucial to anticipating trends that can create or destroy value.

One of the essential pillars is to reconsider how to use new features to improve the way customers are attended. This is based on the obsession with understanding each step of a customer's buying journey, regardless of the channel, and analyzing how digital resources can design and deliver the best experience possible across the enterprise. Since supply chain interaction is a key to delivering the right product efficiently, the way the customer wants, using data and metrics can find information about the customers who, in turn, drive the marketing and sales decisions. This process involves a cyclical dynamic in which processes and capabilities are constantly evolving, based on customer input, promoting permanent loyalty to the product or service.

Swanton and Lehong (2017) detail that when it comes to digital business, targeting aspects of customer value creation, companies can optimize existing business models or transform themselves by creating a business model. An enhanced customer experience is not delivered simply by focusing on the customer interface but is delivered by focusing on multiple platforms in executing a customer-focused strategy.

2.2.2 Digital Transformation

A study presented by Press (2016) reveals that in 2019, global spending on digital transformation initiatives will reach $2.2 trillion, almost 60% more than that spent in 2016. It is rather arduous for traditional companies that already have a structure and form, the task of overcoming the obstacles of their own style and organizational structure, in addition to finding the right talents and strengthening them, adapting their traditional environment into an environment that allows agility in the creation of prototypes, rapid decision-making, and even acceptance because these issues determine whether they can compete in the new digital markets.

According to Downes and Nunes (2013), as a result of this restructuring, whole business models can be reformulated or replaced. Because of this broad scope and far-reaching consequences, digital transformation strategies seek to coordinate efforts to transform products, processes, and organizational aspects due to new technologies, with a more broadly designed scope that explicitly includes digital activities in the interface or totally close to the customers.

Digital business transformation is the application of technology for building new business models, processes, software, and systems that result in more profitable revenue, greater competitive advantage, and greater efficiency (CISCO, 2018). Companies achieve this by transforming business processes and models, enabling workforce efficiency and innovation, and customizing client/citizen experiences (Schwertner, 2017).

In the case of digital business, the question of adapting, transforming, and/or replacing the business model is widely contemplated by the studies on the subject (Burton et al., 2018; Dörner and Edelman, 2015; Swanton and Lehong, 2017). Schallmo et al. (2017) present other definitions of digital transformation:

1. "Typing means the complete network of all sectors of the economy and society, as well as the ability to collect relevant information and analyze and translate that information into actions. The changes bring advantages and opportunities, but they create completely new challenges" (Bertschek et al., 2015).

2. Digital transformation is a "business reinvention process to digitize operations and formulate extended relationships with the supply chain. Digital transformation leadership challenge is to reenergize companies that can already succeed to capture the full potential of information technology across the supply chain" (Bowersox et al., 2005).

3. Digital tranformation – the use of technology to radically improve corporate performance or reach – is becoming an important topic for companies around the world. Executives across all industries are using digital advancements such as analytics, mobility, social media, and embedded smart devices – and enhancing the use of traditional technologies such as Enterprise Resource Planning (ERP) – to change customer relationships, internal processes, and value propositions" (Westerman et al., 2011).

4. "Digital transformation is the deliberate and continuous digital evolution of a company, business model, process of idea or methodology, both strategically and tactically" (Mazzone, 2014).

5. "Digital transformation describes the fundamental transformation of the entire business world through the establishment of new technologies based on the Internet with a fundamental impact on society" (PwC, 2013).

6. "We understand digital transformation as a consistent network of all sectors of the economy and the adjustment of actors to the new realities of the digital economy. Decisions

in networked systems include exchange and analysis of data, calculation and evaluation of options, as well as the initiation of actions and the introduction of consequences" (Bouée and Schaible, 2015).

Schallmo et al. (2017), based on a broad bibliographical query, propose the following approach: Digital transformation includes the network of actors as companies and clients in all segments of the value-added chain and the application of new technologies, requiring skills that involve extraction and exchange of data as well as the analysis and conversion of this data into actions. Information should be used to calculate and evaluate options in order to allow decisions and/or initiate activities in order to increase the performance and reach of a company. Digital transformation involves companies, businesses, models, processes, relationships, products, etc.

2.2.3 Agile Methodology

Having the customer as a central focus means that business processes need to be adapted to meet expectations in a timely manner.

In line with this thinking, and as IT and development become critical to the business, the suitability of these processes for the new delivery time shifts away from traditional methodology and falls into another approach: agile methodologies.

For Highsmith and Cockburn (2001), traditional approaches assumed that with much dedication and efforts they could anticipate the full set of requirements and reduce costs by eliminating change. Today, eliminating change means not responding to dynamic business conditions, not serving the customer in a timely manner, and probably driving the business to failure.

The traditional approach to continuous measurement, error identification, and process refinements struggled to eliminate process change requests, as these variations are the result of errors. Although process problems are caused by some errors, external environmental changes are primarily responsible for the critical variations. Because these changes cannot be eliminated, reducing their cost of response is the most viable strategy rather than eliminating rework.

Expectations have grown over the years, and the market increasingly demands companies to respond to the demands with innovation and high quality.

Agile methodologies are a response to this expectation. Its strategy is to reduce the cost of change over a project.

According to Hoda et al. (2011), agile software development methods emerged in the late 1990s. The agile term was adopted to classify methodologies such as Scrum, XP (Extreme Programming), Crystal, Feature-Driven Development (FDD), Dynamic Software Development Method (DSDM), and Adaptive Software Development.

Agile methods argue that the level of collaboration between the team and its clients is high.

In 2001, in Utah, 17 people, including XP, Scrum, DSDM, among others, and supporters met to discuss new ways to handle software development processes more efficiently and easily. From this meeting came the Agile Manifesto of "Software Development," establishing common principles shared by all these methods (Highsmith, 2001).

The Agile Manifesto has 12 principles with a focus on meeting customer needs, such as: "Our highest priority is to satisfy the customer through continuous and early delivery of value-added software. […] Agile processes take advantage of change for competitive advantage for the customer. […] "

What is new about agile methods is not the practices used, but the recognition of people as the main drivers of project success, along with an intense focus on effectiveness and maneuverability. This produces a new combination of values and principles that defines an "agile" worldview.

2.2.4 Business Model

When we talk about digital companies, the issue of adaptation, transformation, and/or replacement of the business model is widely contemplated by studies on the subject (Burton et al., 2018; Dörner and Edelman, 2015; Swanton and Lehong, 2017).

According to Veit et al. (2014), in a content where business and society undergo extensive digitalization, the logic offered by the business model becomes essential for success, and a subject of great interest to the academic community.

With the digital age, what becomes critical to the success of the business is the availability of adequate levels of information and knowledge. Organizations need to adapt to survive and succeed as their domains, processes, and business technologies change in a world of increasing environmental complexity. Improving your competitive positions, improving your ability to respond quickly to rapid environmental changes with high-quality business decisions, can be supported by the adoption of business models appropriate for this new digital business world (Al-Debi et al., 2008).

The importance of the business model has also been highlighted in the study by Zott et al. (2011) where the authors state that since 1995 there have been at least 1,177 articles published in peer-reviewed academic journals, in which the notion of business model is addressed.

Osterwalder and Pigneur (2010) describe the business model as something that clarifies the logic of creating, delivering, and capturing value in an organization's vision, translated through nine core components segregated into four main areas: business, customers, infrastructure, and financial:

- Client's segment: defines the different groups of people or organizations that a company seeks to reach and serve.
- Value proposition: aggregation or set of benefits that a company offers its clients.
- Channels: the means by which the company communicates and reaches its customer segments to deliver a value proposition.
- Relationship with customers: it establishes the types of relations to be kept with its segments of clients.
- Revenue sources: represents the compensation generated by the customer segment for the delivery of the value.
- Key resources: resources needed to make the business model work.
- Key activities: describes the most important actions that a company must take to make the business model work.
- Main partnerships: network of main suppliers and partners.
- Cost structure: related to all costs involved in the operation.

In more complex and sometimes unique digital businesses, the business model needs to be explicit and provide a new layer of information and knowledge essential to support digital business managers (Al-Debi et al., 2008).

According to Brousseau and Pénard (2007), with the evolution of digital business, it becomes easier to identify the commonalities between the business models that exploded with the growth of the Internet and those that existed before. The new models combine new and innovative ways of organizing the relationship between demand and supply with a pricing strategy that considers network externalities, information specificity, and the ability to differentiate and discriminate through digital technologies.

These new business models contradict the prediction of a massive disintermediation caused by the strong development of digital technologies and the Internet, due to the fact that the intermediaries in this context combine demand and supply plans, then carry out transactions that remain costly within the process. They also perform the combination of various digital products to take advantage of their interoperation – as is the case when content is processed by software running a technical interface – is certainly much easier than it was in the past, thanks to standardized interfaces. However, resource and time expenditures are still required to ensure effective interoperability between digital products to generate a service that adds value to customers. Another reason is related to the availability of goods and services both "on-" and "off-line," making it still a challenge, ensuring the users' access to the information or the specific knowledge they need. Those who can provide the information should receive appropriate incentives as well as potential users should have access to that information.

Kuebel and Zarnekow (2014) have implemented and described a framework for platform business models based on the concepts presented by Al-Debei and Avison (2010) where they identified the value proposition, architecture, network, and finance as the main elements to be examined in the design, analysis, and evaluation of business models (Kuebel and Zarnekow, 2014; see Figure 2.1).

Parker et al. (2017) still define two types of business models for digital companies: pipelines and platforms. For authors, pipelines are more traditional systems employed in most companies that follow a step-by-step

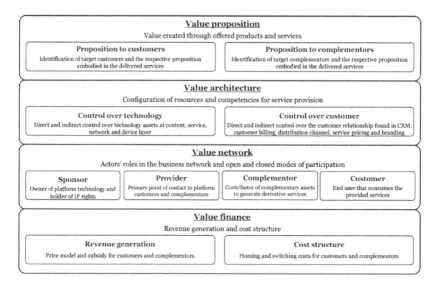

Figure 2.1   Derived analysis framework for platform business models.

scheme that creates value and transfers that value to producers at one end and consumers at another, that is, a linear product chain.

The platform is described as a business that enables an interaction between suppliers and external buyers, creating value for both sides. It provides an environment that creates an infrastructure that encourages interactions, facilitating the exchange of goods, services, or "social currencies."

Many of the Internet success stories – E-Bay, Amazon, Google, Yahoo, Autobytel – have developed business models based on the concept of platforms, assembling components, then grouping them into packages that match complex and specific consumer needs.

To support and better understand the subject, bibliographical research was elaborated on the main themes involved that were digital companies, digital transformation, agile methodology, and business models, which composed the phase of the theoretical framework (foundation). For this stage, national and international scientific knowledge bases such as Web of Science, Elsevier, IEEE, among others, as well as books and other information sites were considered.

In relation to the instruments and protocols used, that is, the form and the mechanisms used to construct and collect the empirical data, interviews with specialists of companies that act strongly in projects of digital transformation in clients of various sizes and segments were used as sources of data. The interviews were conducted with open questions, with a semi-structured script.

The main instrument for organizing and extracting the information chosen is the content analysis performed in the transcript of interviews.

Bardin (1977) describes content analysis as a communication analysis technique, studying the context of what was exposed in the interviews or observed by the researcher, and classifying the material into large subjects or categories, helping in a deep understanding of the exposed material. For the author, content analysis has the following objectives: overcoming uncertainty, hoping with this method to see more clearly the content of materials, and the enrichment of reading, bringing from the detailed analysis, relevant and more enlightening information.

A proposed analysis, suggested by Bardin (1977), can be divided into pre-analysis, material exploration, and treatment of results.

The material must be organized, selected, and eventually hypotheses must be formulated that can be confirmed or refuted during the studies. Some rules must be followed; for example, exhaustiveness, that is, the subject must be exhausted without omissions; representativeness, that is, a sample should represent the chosen universe; homogeneity, that is, subjects should be related to the same theme and collected using similar and equivalent technique and individuals; pertinence, that is, choice of documents should be related to the research objective and exclusivity; and elements should be classified into more than one category.

As a method, Bardin (1977) suggests a general reading and coding of data (absolute or relative frequency), choice of record units, either in word or phrase. Analysis of the frequency at which these registration units appear, and categorization and schematization is aimed at understanding their relevance to the researched subject.

The following sequence was used in the process of this research, composing of:

- A general reading of the interviews.
- Categorization of the essential items for the study into domains, subcategories, and categories.

- Analysis of frequency and relevance within the material.
- Identification and correlation with national and international academic literature.

The data obtained from the content analysis are aligned with the theoretical foundation. The categories – difficulties, processes, and technologies – offer insight into characteristics, while business model meets the peculiarities of strategy, referring to the framework presented by Kuebel and Zarnekow (2014) that identifies the value proposition, architecture, network, and finance as the "main elements to be examined in the design, analysis, and evaluation of business models" (Al-Debei and Avison, 2010).

2.3 Results and Analysis

2.3.1 Interviews

2.3.1.1 Analysis 1   The first expert interviewed works in an Indian multinational company that operates in Brazil with several fronts such as technology and service design. The company has a strong technological aspect in its operations but sought to acquire other complementary companies that would bring a more consultative vision to understand, not only the technological issue but the business as a whole, supported by these technologies, thus allowing to attend the cycle all for digital transformation. It serves companies seeking a renewal or disruption, in some cases traditional companies that seek to reinvent themselves.

The interview was held in October 2018, using the Skype tool with digital file recording and later transcribed using Atlas software.

One of the main points raised by the interviewee was the question of understanding the business vision with the centrality of the user, redesigning the process in search of innovation. He also considered that there was a great lack of alignment with the concept of what is digital transformation, and many customers still understand that only investment in technology is enough for a digital transformation of the business. Emphasis was placed on the importance of revisiting processes and aligning strategy and technologies.

In the interview, the question of the processes appears in evidence, and it helps in the understanding of where the company wants to arrive and how and what to do to align the strategy for effectiveness in the digital transformation of the business.

In addition, there have been cases in which customers invest in leading-edge technologies and are involved in the process of digital transformation, but the use of technology in isolation does not transform the business. It is mandatory to align with the other areas so that the data is transformed into information that leads to the expected result strategically.

The issue of culture change is also a priority and preparing teams is critical.

2.3.1.2 Analysis 2 The second expert interviewed works in a Brazilian multinational company that was born as a software consultant and today works mainly with digital transformation. Some clients come from the software consultancy, extending the projects aiming at an evolution toward a true digital transformation, others are already specifically looking for a move to digital.

The interview was held in October 2018, through the phone with digital file recording and later transcribed using Atlas software.

The interviewee stressed that generally a digital transformation project begins with the management part. Predicting the scenarios, the company needs to understand the need for digital transformation within its business and seeks out specialists who can assist it in this transformation. An analysis of the return of this investment, the difficulties, and the necessary time is made, going to the training of the leaders and then arriving in the operational.

It is not possible to do digital transformation in some areas only; it is usually a horizontal process that takes a product and goes through all areas. All the leaders involved are trained this way and can help to clarify internally in the company the importance and benefits of this change.

One premise within digital transformation is the involvement of the ecosystem to minimize risk. With this, the analysis of the company is much more complete, but this process depends on the level of maturity of the company culture. For this to happen, paradigm shattering and culture shock need to be very well worked out.

With this closer involvement of customers and partners, there is a need for companies to respond faster, and this is reflected in internal IT processes. Implementation deadlines should be reduced, and software developments need to adapt to agile cultures, bringing people from infrastructure into teams and automating processes to ensure security and risk minimization. Another aspect is that the owner of the product becomes the owner of the process, assuming the management of production lead times in the time the market demands, generating dynamism in the analysis through automation techniques and control tools for a greater aggregation of value for customers.

When the company's culture changes, digital transformation takes the company to another reality, and it is mandatory to revisit the business model and update it to this new reality. This is a big challenge for traditional companies because for a large company today, a failure can cause millions of losses, but if the business model does not adapt to the agility demanded by the market, competing with the start-ups that arise presenting new solutions that take advantage of their agility can transform the market they enter, that is, they can test their business models quickly and cheaply, changing and adjusting according to the market response; traditional companies can be swallowed and expelled from their current markets.

2.3.1.3 Analysis 3   The third expert has worked for 20 years in a multinational technology company, the last two years focusing on leading teams of experts in digital transformation projects.

The interview was held in October 2018, in person with digital file recording and later transcribed using Atlas software.

Many of the customers did not know what digital transformation was. Start-ups come with a business model and a culture of fast service to customer needs, already structured with agile methodologies for quick response in digital channels.

He considers three types of digital transformation projects: software development, research and development, and innovation.

Digital transformation changes the company's way of doing business and not only involves parts, such as the use of technologies or methodologies. The digital transformation of large traditional companies often involves a phase of living with digital and traditional aspects for a long time. It is necessary to invest in technologies that aggregate and talk with traditional solutions in order to achieve the dynamism of companies already born digital. An example would be cloud solutions.

There is a cultural problem in companies regarding the understanding of digital transformation.

Digital transformation indirectly involves the entire suitability of the company's chain. It needs analysis of its essence with change in every link and a thorough reanalysis of the business model as a whole. Transformation also involves capturing and harnessing information to feed the chain and decision-making.

Digital transformation is more than technology; it is business related. People need to adapt and always be up to date on the best practices and news that come up every day.

Digital transformation is using tools to create new values to deliver to customers. Companies should take this into their strategy and look at ways to achieve it.

2.3.1.4 Interviews Analysis In order to answer which factors companies should focus on in the question of the digital transformation of their business, a summary table was elaborated from the essential points that were presented in the analyses of the interviews (Table 2.1).

Table 2.1 Summary View of the Main Points

	ANALYSIS 1	ANALYSIS 2	ANALYSIS 3
Value offer	The value proposition is in the understanding of what the client wants, concepts and objectives, but the company's own culture does not allow, difficult to understand the value proposition	Customers still do not understand the value proposition; it is still very vague for them. The very understanding that the customer should participate in the process	Not very clear for clients who want to transform the business, as well as many other digital concepts
Value creation	It is in the processes that will be remodeled	In the view of companies the use of business model is mandatory to revisit the business model and update it to this new reality	Digital transformation is using tools to create new values to deliver to customers
Value delivery	Generally, value is economic in the view of companies	Generally, value is economic in the view of companies	Generally, value is economic in the view of companies

(Continued)

Table 2.1 (Continued)   Summary View of the Main Points

	ANALYSIS 1	ANALYSIS 2	ANALYSIS 3
Culture	There is a lack of culture, to be inserted in a broader context	It is time to train the leaders, to implant the digital culture	Very common problem for traditional companies
People/ training	Change the culture, thought	Essential to train people, there is no formal education for this digital environment	All teams need to be always tuned with new technologies and process, align with market tendency
Technology	Without processes and alignment with the vision, strategy does not mean a true digital transformation. There is a need to use technology to capture data and transport information to results linked to strategy	On average, only 30% of a project is related to technology within digital transformation; 60% is the issue of communication and training and disruption of paradigms It needs a set of changes	Technology is just a part of digital transformation. Without a business model review and culture transformation, technology by itself does not characterize a digital transformation.
Processes	Focus change on internal and external customers	It requires an adaptation of current processes to better respond to the market/customers	Adapt the chain to support new time-to-market
Difficulties	Lack of business understanding of what they want. Need for leveling, culture talk, and change management. It requires commitment and takes more time	Breaking the company's internal paradigms, each area looks at its world, and digital transformation requires it to look at the whole, for the product. It is a culture shock	The challenging issue for traditional companies is the convenience between legacy and the new business model
Related issues	Agile methodologies, processes	Agile methodologies, lean, culture	Agile methodologies

2.4 Conclusion

The objectives of this project were reached in the expert opinions on the digital transformation, important issues about digital transformation. It can be concluded that the factors pointed out by the interviewees converge to what the literature cites: There is a need to review the business models of companies comprehensively; the introduction of new technologies must be accompanied by restructuring of production processes, people management and changes, introduction of agile methods, and ways of communicating internally and externally.

It is very important for traditional companies to consider a process that supports the new time-to-market; it includes new people skills, methodologies, and culture transformation without forgetting hard interaction between legacy and new technologies.

These services of digital business platforms, business platforms or shared economy, have great adhesion due to the ease of use and the quality of the services offered, identified in the texts the clear presence of the concept of offered value that induces the concept of value creation.

Acknowledgment

This work is funded by FAPESP (Foundation for Research Support of the State of São Paulo), through the project "New technological ecosystems in productive systems: A review and research agenda for digital business platforms."

References

Al-Debei, M.M., Avison, D. (2010). Developing a unified framework of the business model concept. *European Journal of Information Systems*, *19(3)*, pp. 359–376.

Al-Debi, M.M., El-Haddadeh, R., Avison, D. (2008). *Defining the business model in the new world of digital business.* AMCIS 2008 Proceedings, pp. 1-11.

Bardin, L. (1977). Análise de conteúdo. Luis Antero Reto e Augusto Pinheiro. *Edições, 70.*

Bertschek, I., Clement, R., Buhr, D., Hirsch-Kreinsen, H., Falck, O., Heimisch, A., Jacob-Puchalska, A., Mazat, A. (2015). Industrie 4.0: Digitale Wirtschaft–Herausforderung und chance für Unternehmen und Arbeitswelt. *Ifo Schnelldienst, 68(10)*, pp. 3–18.

Bouée, C.E., Schaible, S. (2015). *Die Digitale Transformation der Industrie.* Berlin: Roland Berger Strategy Consultans und Bundesverband der Deutschen Industrie eV.

Bowersox, D.J., Closs, D.J., Drayer, R.W. (2005). The digital transformation: Technology and beyond. *Supply Chain Management Review, 9(1)*, pp. 22–29.

Brousseau, E., Pénard, T. (2007). The economics of digital business models: A framework for analyzing the economics of platforms. *Review of Network Economics, 6(2)* pp. 81–116.

Burton, B., Scheibenreif, D., Barnes, H., Smith, M., Buytendijk, F., Bradley A. (2018). Digital business gives rise to the new economics of connections. McKinsey & Company Article. Gartner, Inc. Retrieved from: http://www.gartner.com/imagesrv/research/algorithm-economy/pdf/algorithm-economy-292457.pdf. (Access: 27.05.2018).

CISCO. (2018). Retrieved from: https://discover.cisco.com/en/us/digital-business/whitepaper/transformation/introduction-626F-200PY.html. (Access: 01.12. 2018).

Chew, K. (2015). Digital organizations of the future. In: J. Collin, K. Hiekkanen, J.J. Korhonen, M. Halén, T. Itälä, M. Helenius (eds.), *IT leadership in transition: The impact of digitalization on Finnish organizations*. Helsinki: Aalto University School of Science.

Dörner, K., Edelman, D. (2015). *What digital really means*. McKinsey & Company Article. Retrieved from: https://www.mckinsey.com/industries/high-tech/our-insights/what-digital-really-means. (Access: 09.05.2018).

Downes, L., Nunes, P. (2013). Blockbuster becomes a casualty of big bang disruption. *Harvard Business Review, 7*.

Highsmith, J. (2001). *Manifesto Ágil*. Retrieved from: http://agilemanifesto.org/history.html. (Access: 10.05.2018).

Highsmith, J., Cockburn, A. (2001). Agile software development: The business of innovation. *Computer, 34(9)*, pp. 120–127.

Hoda, R., Noble, J., Marshall, S. (2011). The impact of inadequate customer collaboration on self-organizing agile teams. *Information and Software Technology, 53(5)*, pp. 521–534.

Itälä, T. (2015). Digital business and platforms. In: J. Collin, K. Hiekkanen, J.J. Korhonen, M. Halén, T. Itälä, M. Helenius (eds.), *IT leadership in transition: The impact of digitalization on Finnish organizations*. Helsinki: Aalto University School of Science.

Kane, G.C., Palmer, D., Phillips, A.N., Kiron, D., Buckley, N. (2015). Strategy, not technology, drives digital transformation. *MIT Sloan Management Review and Deloitte University Press, 14(1–25)*.

Kuebel, H., Zarnekow, R. (2014). *Evaluating platform business models in the telecommunications industry via framework*. Twentieth Americas Conference on Information Systems, Savannah.

Llorente, J.A. (2016). A transformação digital. *Revista Uno, 24*. Retrieved from: https://www.revista-uno.com.br/numero-24/a-transformacao-digital/. (Access: 20.08.2018).

Mazzone, D.M. (2014). *Digital or death: Digital transformation: The only choice for business to survive smash and conquer*. Smashbox Consulting Inc.

Osterwalder, A., Pigneur, Y. (2010). *Business model canvas*. Self-Published. Last.

Parker, G.G., Van Alstyne, M.W., Choudary, S.P. (2017). *Plataforma: A revolução da estratégia*. São Paulo: Casa Educação.

Press, G. (2016). Top 10 Tech predictions for 2017 from IDC. *Forbes*. Retrieved from: https://www.forbes.com/sites/gilpress/2016/11/01/top-10-tech-predictions-for-2017-from-idc/#1bf2833d4aad. (Access: 25.08.2018).

PwC. (2013). *Digitale Transformation – der größte Wandel seit der Industriellen Revolution*. Frankfurt: PricewaterhouseCoopers.

Schallmo, D., Williams, C.A., Boardman, L. (2017). Digital transformation of business models—Best practice, enablers, and roadmap. *International Journal of Innovation Management*, *21(08)*, p. 1740014.

Schwertner, K. (2017). Digital transformation of business. *Trakia Journal of Sciences*, *15(1)*, pp. 388–393.

Swanton, B., Lehong, H. (2017). *A digital business technology platform is fundamental to scaling digital business*. Gartner, Inc.

Turban, E., King, D., Lee, J.K., Liang, T.P., Turban, D.C. (2015). *Electronic commerce: A managerial and social networks perspective*, (Rev. ed.). Switzerland: Springer International Publishing.

Veit, D., Clemons, E., Benlian, A., Buxmann, P., Hess, T., Kundisch, D., Leimeister, J.M., Loos, P., Spann, M. (2014). Business models. *Business & Information Systems Engineering*, *6(1)*, pp. 45–53.

Westerman, G., Calméjane, C., Bonnet, D., Ferraris, P., McAfee, A. (2011). *Digital transformation: A roadmap for billion-dollar organization*. MITSloan Management Review.

Zott, Ch., Amit, R., Massa, L. (2011). The business model: Recent developments and future research. *Journal of Management*, *37(4)*, pp. 1019–1042.

3

Value Composition for Business Models of High-Growth Enterprises

IWONA OTOLA,
MARLENA GRABOWSKA, AND
MAREK SZAJT

Contents

3.1 Introduction

In the literature, the number of studies on high-growth enterprises (HGEs) is increasing. HGEs affect the development of the economy not only through their own development, but also through the creation of new jobs and an innovative approach to doing business. HGEs operate in all sectors and incorporate all company sizes, however, the most of them can be observed among small and young enterprises (Daunfeldt et al., 2016; Demir et al., 2017). However, most of the problems arise when determining what criteria are adequate to name an enterprise an HGEs. Currently, it is widely accepted that HGEs are characterized by an increase in revenues from sales or the employment of more than 20% on average annually over the consecutive three years (OECD, 2010). Microeconomic studies on HGEs focus on the potential to create jobs (Coad et al., 2014), processes, forecasts, and conditions that make companies' development easier or harder (McKelvie and Wiklund, 2010).

From the economic development point of view, HGEs are important, because they create jobs and belong to the group of innovative enterprises; in addition, they quickly react to changes in the market and adapt to its requirements. This quick response to changes is reflected in HGEs' business models (BMs). This is particularly important in the current economic situation, where changes in the labor market tendencies are observed, caused by the displacement of the employer market by the employee market. Any well-operating enterprise bases its activity not only on developed long-time strategy but most of all on the BMs. The ability to create BMs is an important issue for entrepreneurs. The way they create their BM is determined, for example, by the income level or competitive position on the market. HGEs should be a reference point for other entities, as their BMs are characterized by the employment increase and/or sales revenues increase. It is worth to take a closer look at how HGEs build their BMs.

3.2 Elements of the Business Model Construction

The issue of constructing BMs is already quite widespread in theoretical and practical researches. The functioning of the enterprise must be based on a specific action logic. In any economic entity, it is necessary to determine the ways that reflect the concept of its activity and at the same time illustrate the methods of achieving the assumed goals. Creating an original business idea obliges to undertake further projects determining the scheme of further functioning of the enterprise. The enterprise's activity must be carried out according to specific assumptions. Creating a tool that schematically illustrates the idea of business and reflects the business plan is linked to building a BM. Bearing in mind that the model is a simplified picture of reality, it can be pointed out that the BM is a simplified picture of the business reality, and thus a pattern of business activities.

The idea of the BM is to determine the path of an enterprise development as well as operational level activities that would make this activity profitable and ensure the increase in the enterprise value. The environment, where the modern enterprises operate, is characterized with strong dynamics and complexity, thus requires the enterprise management to accept and understand the changes and be flexible in their activities. Even if the existing BM provides assumed benefits, it should be remembered that changes in the environment may support new opportunities and challenges (Chesbrough, 2006, p.81). Subsequently, this requires constant verification and adaptation of existing BM to changes in the market environment (Otola and Grabowska, 2018).

There is no single universal BM for all enterprises. Each type of business activity requires an individual approach to answering the key questions: What do we want to do, who is our customer, how do we want to provide our services/products, how do we make profit. Operating conditions for business entities impose the need to introduce innovation into various areas and spheres of enterprise activity. However, the design of future BM as well as the improvement of an existing one that adapts it to ever-changing environment, both require a set of conceptual tools (Zott and Amit, 2010). A well-constructed BM is based on many different components. The subject literature presents many methods for the BM construction, and each of them is based on components considered crucial by the idea creator. The most popular conceptual tool for developing an individual BM is the Business Model Canvas (BMC) created by Osterwalder et al. (2005), whose nine basic blocks can be classified into three general categories: revenue/product aspects, business actor and network aspects, and marketing-specific aspects. Table 3.1 presents the BM elements that are the most popular in the literature.

Research on BMs so far has been related either to conceptual approaches to the model itself (Afuah and Tucci, 2000; Amit and Zott, 2001; Morris et al., 2005; Osterwalder et al., 2005; Richardson, 2008; Teece, 2010) or empirical (mostly case study) indications of these models (e.g., Chesbrough, 2006; Landau et al., 2016; Solaimani et al., 2018; Spieth and Schneider, 2016). Despite the fact that BM conceptual approaches differ, primarily in the number of components, it is worth mentioning that many of them have common elements. However, the attention should be paid not only to BM components, but most of all to relations between them. It is impossible to create a successful BM, where each component is designed properly, but there is no synergy effect between the components. Some of the

Table 3.1   Business Model Elements

AUTHORS	BM COMPONENTS
Chesbrough and Rosenbloom (2002)	Value proposition Target markets Internal value chain structure Cost structure and profit model Value network Competitive strategy
Alt and Zimmermann (2001)	Mission Structure Processes Revenues Legal issues Technology
Afuah and Tucci (2000)	Customer value Scope Price Revenue Connected activities Implementation Capabilities Sustainability
Amit and Zott (2001)	Design elements: transaction content, transaction structure, transaction governance Design themes: novelty, lock-in, complementarities, efficiency
Osterwalder et al. (2005)	Value proposition Customer segments Key partners Delivery channels Revenue streams Key resources Key activities Customer relationship Cost structure
Tikkanen et al. (2005)	Company's network of relationships The resource base and business process operations Finance and accounting aspects of the company
Richardson (2008)	Value proposition Value creation and delivery system Value capture
Demil and Lecocq (2010)	Resources and competences Organization Value propositions
Zhang et al. (2016)	Core products Target market Operation procedure Value allocation principle Value chain structure

few publications in the subject literature that identify the relations between individual BM components are the BMC by Osterwalder et al. (2005) and the evolutionary BM proposed by Tikkanen et al. (2005). BMC is a template that does not impose any particular starting point for the analysis of a given undertaking. Its ultimate purpose is to provide the user with a clear understanding of the organization uniqueness and the way in which it satisfies the needs of target customers by focusing on possible relations among its nine components (Nielsen and Roslender, 2015). In the case of the model proposed by Tikkanen et al. (2005), there is an interaction between tangible BM elements (strategy and structure, network, operations, finance, and accounting) and managerial cognition (structures or the belief system of a company). According to the authors, first, significant relations should appear between tangible elements, as the lack of convergence between them might lead to the failure of developed BM. Second, relations between tangible elements and managers responsible for individual components are important. This approach indicates that BM is a cognitive mechanism. It is also worth mentioning the BM proposed by J. Richardson (2008), which does not directly indicate relations between BM components, but its assumed ultimate result, that is, value capture, which then translates into an enterprise competitive position. The author believes that a well-designed BM creates a holistic view of the enterprise activities in order to implement the strategy. It supports the management in determining a logically coherent structure of activities to create and deliver value added. Therefore, the main BM components are based on values:

- Value proposition – referring to the identification of target customers and the description of what is offered to customers.
- Creation and delivery system of value – that is, indicating the processes and activities including the resources involved that participate in the value chain.
- Capture of value – answering why a specific BM is profitable, with the use of the analysis of enterprise revenue and cost structure.

The model outlined with the above elements (value proposition, value creation and delivery system, and value capture) is an instrument of value composition.

Value composition is present in all second-order BM elements described in its framework and including among others unique structure of activities and resources, and innovative value proposition for customers, as well as a scheme of capturing and allocating economic value (Teece, 2010; Tallman et al., 2018).

The first element, that is value proposition, primarily focuses on the customer and satisfying his potential needs. It is a set of benefits offered to customers. It is characterized by multidimensionality, manifested in various aspects of offered benefits in terms of quality, reliability, availability, throughput, or status (Biloshapka and Osiyevskyy, 2018; Sheehan and Bruni-Bossio, 2015). The priority determinant of value proposition is a precise identification of the target group, which the enterprise offer is directed to, including the indication of key customers. From the target group's point of view, it is justified and significant for the company to present a unique product/service to a potential recipient. Such an offer distinguishes a given company on the market among its competition. The importance of the isolating mechanism that blocks and prevents competitors from instant imitating is crucial (Teece, 2010). The value proposition also indicates relations of the company with its partners, understood as customers and suppliers, as well as factors that are important elements of these relations.

The second element is value creation and delivery system, which includes the most partial components, that is, resources and capabilities, key activities, value chain, and business processes. According to Tallman (2014), value creation equals the process that allocates resources and capabilities of the enterprise to the needs and expectations demanded by the customers in such a way that is better than the other possible ways. Also, the same author understands value delivery as a logistic process connecting the company's organizational structure with the structure of markets in which that company operates. The definition of the enterprise key resources and capabilities should focus on determining which assets are indispensable to maintain the business process. On the other hand, key activities highlight the most important activities contributing to the proper and efficient operation of the business process. However, a significant element that affects the value creation and delivery system is the value chain. Information, sale, and distribution channels should be designed and arranged in a way that supports an effective and efficient value delivery to customers.

The last element of BM is value capture, which aims at outlining future incomes that ensure profit margin in relation to planned costs (Richardson, 2008). The process of value capture enables the company to get a part of the value that was created for customers in the form of economic rents, excess profits, or cash flows (Tallman et al., 2018). Value capture determines all types of revenues that can be generated by the model as well as costs that are incurred in the entire business process. A special attention should be paid to financial expenditures in relation to key resources, key activities, and the cooperation with partners. An important aspect is also an accurate estimation of fixed and variable costs with the allowance for possible areas of their future reduction, as well as the indication of possible extra cost areas that may emerge due to the activities planned. In addition, it is crucial to determine for which services/products a customer is willing to pay, and which should be delivered without charging the customer. When assessing value capture for the enterprise from suppliers and customers, some comparisons with other suppliers and customers should also be made (Bowman and Ambrosini, 2000).

It is worth noticing that the value composition based on *value proposition*, *value creation and delivery system*, and *value capture* does not consist only in the internal value generation, but also in negotiating value propositions with customers, partners, and suppliers that come with different requirements, ever changing under various factors (Tallman, 2014). The above-presented considerations on BM elements require a remark stating that each of these elements plays a crucial role in the process of enterprise value composition, but not each of them participates in the process in the same degree (Zhang et al., 2016). Summing up, there are elements dominating in the BM that are of key importance for the value composition process.

3.3 Value Composition in HGEs Business Models – Empirical Researches

What distinguishes some enterprises from others is the success they achieve. Given that HGEs have succeeded, it seems appropriate to analyze their BMs, which allows to find their common features. However, the analytical concept selected this way does not negate the individuality and originality of the BM implemented in a given business entity, but only refers to presenting components that were of key importance in the BM. It is important to be able to verify a BM proposed by a company, using performance measures. Testing how individual BM components affect the selected performance measures allows to determine which of them are significant for company value composition. The measurement of relations between elements highlighted in proposed BM was made on the basis of structural equation modelling (SEM). The choice of this method was determined by the complex structure of the model. The advantage of this method is therefore the possibility to test research hypotheses with great complexity of relations between variables, by including latent variables in addition to measured variables in the model.

Empirical research was conducted at the beginning of 2019 using a questionnaire survey on a group of 100 HGEs in Poland. HGEs were identified as those which increase in revenues from sales or the employment scored more than 20% on average annually over the consecutive three years. Enterprises that met one of the above conditions were included in the research.

Empirical research on value composition used the assumptions of BM construction proposed by J. Richardson (2008). Based on three main elements, that is, value proposition, value creation and delivery system, and value capture, three theoretical constructs were created, namely, *value proposition, value creation and delivery system*, and *value capture*. Each of these constructs is very complex and may be illustrated by various components. It was assumed that a given construct is made of a group of specific factors – variables (the so-called measured variables) related to a given value component. Factors included in individual theoretical constructs and their relations are presented in Figure 3.1.

Ten measured variables were distinguished in the group of *value proposition*. Some of them are related to the enterprise partners, that is, key customer, recipient, and supplier (x1–x5). Factors affecting the enterprise relation with the key supplier were also isolated (x6.1–x6.5). In the group of *value creation and delivery system* 32 measured variables were distinguished that may be classified into six groups: main products/services (y1.1–y1.5), resources from key suppliers (y2.1–y2.5), enterprise key activity (y3.1–y3.5), resource key categories (y4.1–y4.4), significant groups of intangible resources (y5.1–y5.7),

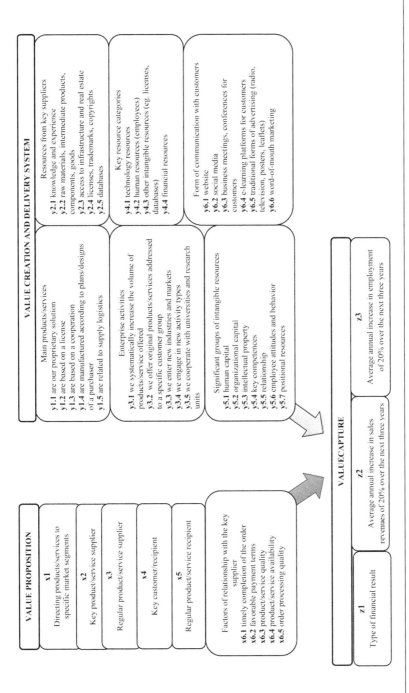

Figure 3.1   BM theoretical constructs and their factors.

and form of customer communication (y6.1–y6.6). *Value capture* group of variables is responsible for BM profitability, thus three variables were included: type of financial result (z1), increase in sales revenues (z2), and increase in employment (z3).

In the proposed model, the theoretical constructs (latent variables) *value proposition* and *value creation and delivery system* affect the theoretical construct (latent variable) *value capture*. This approach indicates that a properly constructed *value proposition* in a BM should contribute to *value capture* as well as a well-constructed *value creation and delivery system* should have a positive effect on *value capture*.

In the course of the research, the statistical significance of relations between the exogenous variables, distinguished in the model and the endogenous variable, considered from the perspective of BM value composition, was determined. The constructions were identified, where the relation of latent variables *value proposition* and *value creation and delivery system* to the latent variable *value capture* was statistically significant. The holistic nature of the research results from the allowance, after determining exogenous and endogenous variables, for all measured variables identified in survey questions.

Based on the research, key determinants for the construction of high-growth enterprises business models were indicated. Figure 3.2 presents the path model of the effect of latent variables *value proposition* and *value creation and delivery system* on the latent variable *value capture* including the effect of individual measured variables on latent variables for the examined research group.

Based on the above data, a statistically significant effect of theoretical constructs *value proposition, value creation and delivery system* on the theoretical construct *value capture* can be indicated. The strength of this relation can be described as positive and medium-level. Out of the ten measured variables identified in the study for the latent variable *value proposition*, five variables are statistically significant. In this case, the strongest positive effect on the theoretical construct *value proposition* is exerted by having a key customer – recipient (x4), by emphasizing the quality of production and services (x6.3), and by having regular recipients of products and services (x5). Directing products/services to specific market segments (x1) and having regular suppliers of products/services (x3) were also important for *value proposition*. Thirty-two measured variables identified for the latent variable *value*

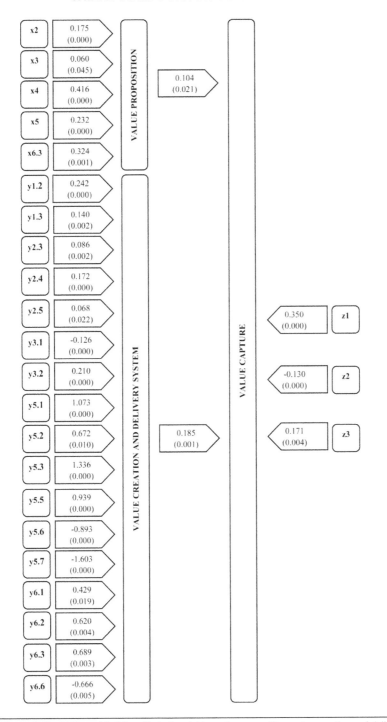

Figure 3.2 Path model of the effect of variables value proposition, value creation and delivery system, and value capture.

creation and delivery system, demonstrated 17 that were confirmed as statistically significant. The strongest positive effect was found for variables classified into the group of intangible resources, such as intellectual property (y5.3), relationships (y5.5), organizational capital (y5.2), and human capital (y5.1). Also, a high rank was given to factors from the group in the form of communication with customers. The factors having a significant effect such as business meetings and conferences for customers (y6.3), use of social media (y6.2), and websites (y6.1) should be highlighted. In addition, it is worth paying attention to following factors from the group of resources from key suppliers: licenses, trademarks, copyrights (y2.4), access to infrastructure and real estate (y2.3), and databases (y2.5). Therefore, it can be indicated that in the research sample, the increase in value creation and proposition factors favors the increase in value capture. All three measured variables being studied can be considered as statistically significant factors of *value capture*. The greatest effect is assigned to the measured variable z1, representing the appropriate (positive) financial result in over the longest possible time. The positive effect on *value capture* is also exerted by the measured variable z3 defined as the increase in employment exceeding 20% on average annually over the last three years. Finally, the negative effect on *value capture* was observed for the measured variable z2 reflecting the increase in sales revenues exceeding 20% on average annually over the last three years.

The effect of both latent variables *value proposition* (0.104) and *value creation and delivery system* (0.185) in surveyed enterprises proved to be weak, but statistically significant.

3.4 Conclusion

The theoretical considerations carried out above indicate heterogeneous yet similar forms of BM construction. Our concept refers to BM based on the process of value composition that incorporates three significant first-order elements: *value proposition, value creation and delivery system*, and *value capture*. This choice was dictated by the assumption of BM profitability, which is best considered in terms of value. Value composition is important for a well-developed BM. Our research confirmed the theoretical assumptions on *value proposition*, the element which strongly emphasized the customer and satisfying his/her needs. There is a noticeable difference between perceiving relations with customers and suppliers and establishing links to their partners. Both key and regular customers are important for a company, but in the case of a supplier, this partner should be regular, not necessarily key. No significant importance for HGEs was observed for such factors related to key supplier, that is, timely completion of the order, favorable payment terms, product/service availability, and order processing quality. In relation to *value creation and delivery system*, variables from the group of intangible resources proved to be the most significant among all proposed factors that were examined. A special attention was also paid to resources from key suppliers. In HGEs BMs, the *value creation and delivery system* is mostly based on the form of communication with customers. The research results confirmed that information channels are an important element of effective and efficient way of delivering value to customers. However, no significant effect on *value creation and delivery system* was observed for such elements as key activities and key resources. Our theoretical construct *value capture* was designed differently from its presentation in the subject literature. We did not focus on the income and cost model, but adopted assumptions related to the definition approach to HGEs. The conducted research allows to state that statistically significant factors distinguished in constructs *value proposition* and *value creation and delivery system* exert an effect on *value capture*, and therefore confirm the validity of constructing BM based on the process of value composition.

References

Afuah, A., Tucci, C.L. (2000). *Internet business models and strategies: Text and cases*. Boston: McGraw-Hill Higher Education.

Alt, R., Zimmermann, H. (2001). Introduction to special section business models. *Electronic Markets, 11(1)*, pp. 3–9.

Amit, R., Zott, C. (2001). Value creation in e-business. *Strategic Management Journal, 22(6–7)*, pp. 493–520.

Biloshapka, V., Osiyevskyy, O. (2018). Value creation mechanisms of business models: Proposition, targeting, appropriation, and delivery. *The International Journal of Entrepreneurship and Innovation, 19(3)*, pp. 166–176.

Bowman, C., Ambrosini, V. (2000). Value creation versus value capture: Towards a coherent definition of value in strategy. *British Journal of Management, 11(1)*, pp. 1–15.

Chesbrough, H. (2006). *Open business models: How to thrive in the new innovation landscape.* Boston: Harvard Business Press.

Chesbrough, H., Rosenbloom, R.S. (2002). The role of the business model in capturing value from innovation: Evidence from Xerox Corporation's technology spin-off companies. *Industrial and Corporate Change, 11(3)*, pp. 529–555.

Coad, A., Daunfeldt, S.O., Johansson, D., Wennberg, K. (2014). Whom do high-growth firms hire? *Industrial and Corporate Change, 23(1)*, pp. 293–327.

Daunfeldt, S.O., Elert, N., Johansson, D. (2016). Are high-growth firms overrepresented in high-tech industries? *Industrial and Corporate Change, 25(1)*, pp. 1–21.

Demil, B., Lecocq, X. (2010). Business model evolution: In search of dynamic consistency. *Long Range Planning, 43(2–3)*, pp. 227–246.

Demir, R., Wennberg, K., McKelvie, A. (2017). The strategic management of high-growth firms: A review and theoretical conceptualization. *Long Range Planning, 50(4)*, pp. 431–456.

Landau, C., Karna, A., Sailer, M. (2016). Business model adaptation for emerging markets: A case study of a German automobile manufacturer in India. *R&D Management, 46(3)*, pp. 480–503.

McKelvie, A., Wiklund, J. (2010). Advancing firm growth research: A focus on growth mode instead of growth rate. *Entrepreneurship Theory and Practice, 34(2)*, pp. 261–288.

Mezger, F. (2014). Toward a capability based conceptualization of business model innovation: Insights from an explorative study. *R&D Management, 44(5)*, pp. 429–449.

Morris, M., Schindehutte, M., Allen, J. (2005). The entrepreneur's business model: Toward a unified perspective. *Journal of Business Research, 58(6)*, pp. 726–735.

Nielsen, C., Roslender, R. (2015). Enhancing financial reporting: The contribution of business models. *The British Accounting Review, 47(3)*, pp. 262–274.

OECD (2010). *High-growth enterprises: What governments can do to make a difference, OECD studies on SMEs and entrepreneurship.* OECD Publishing. Retrieved from: Dx.doi.org/ 10.1787/9789264048782-en. (Access: 15.10.2019).

Osterwalder, A., Pigneur, Y., Tucci, Ch.L. (2005). Clarifying business models: Origins, present, and future of the concept. *Communications of the Association for Information Systems, 16*, pp. 1–25.

Otola, I., Grabowska, M. (2018). Koncepcje budowy modeli biznesu w spółkach sektora informatyka. *Zeszyty Naukowe Politechniki Śląskiej. Organizacja i Zarządzanie*, Nr 130, pp. 193–208.

Richardson, J. (2008). The business model: An integrative framework for strategy execution. *Strategic Change, 17(5–6)*, pp. 133–144.

Sheehan, N.T., Bruni-Bossio, V. (2015). Strategic value curve analysis: Diagnosing and improving customer value propositions. *Business Horizons, 58(3)*, pp. 317–324.

Solaimani, S., Heikkilä, M., Bouwman, H. (2018). Business model implementation within networked enterprises: A case study on a Finnish pharmaceutical project. *European Management Review, 15(1)*, pp. 79–96.

Spieth, P., Schneider, S. (2016). Business model innovativeness: Designing a formative measure for business model innovation. *Journal of Business Economics, 86(6)*, pp. 671–696.

Tallman, S. (2014). Business models and the multinational firm. In: J. Boddewyn (ed.), *Multidisciplinary insights from new AIB fellows*. Bingley, West Yorkshire, UK: Emerald Group Publishing, pp. 115–138.

Tallman, S., Luo, Y., Buckley, P.J. (2018). Business models in global competition. *Global Strategy Journal, 8(4)*, pp. 517–535.

Teece, D.J. (2010). Business models, business strategy and innovation. *Long Range Planning, 43(2–3)*, pp. 172–194.

Tikkanen, H., Lamberg, J.A., Parvinen, P., Kallunki, J.P. (2005). Managerial cognition, action and the business model of the firm. *Management decision, 43(6)*, pp. 789–809.

Zhang, Y., Zhao, S., Xu, X. (2016). Business model innovation: An integrated approach based on elements and functions. *Information Technology and Management, 17(3)*, pp. 303–310.

Zott, C., Amit, R. (2010). Business model design: An activity system perspective. *Long Range Planning, 43(2–3)*, pp. 216–226.

4

THE VARIETY OF ASPECTS OF BUSINESS MODELS IN THE HIGH-GROWTH AND HIGH-TECH ENTERPRISES: AN ESTONIAN CASE

PIIA VETTIK-LEEMET,
MERVI RAUDSAAR, AND
MERIKE KASEORG

Contents

4.1 Introduction

The relevance of the business model in relation to the enterprise's performance, in general, has been widely acknowledged in literature. On one hand, the business model approach is increasingly addressing the business model as an economic concept, which "produces" revenues and costs (Slávik and Bednár, 2014). On the other hand, there is a growing body of literature that provides a range of approaches to characterizing their different components in achieving global growth (Chesbrough, 2003, 2006, 2010; Osterwalder and Pigneur, 2009; Teece, 2010; Watson, 2006).

This stream of the literature also tries to distinguish business model components and functions (Afuah, 2004; Chesbrough, 2003, 2006; Osterwalder and Pigneur, 2009; Teece, 2010; Watson, 2006). The business model and its components are becoming even more important in the changing economic environment, where the main emphasis is being put on knowledge-based start-ups in the high-growth and high-tech realms. The purpose of this chapter is to conceptualize the differences between a variety of business models and their components and identify differences between mainstream, high-tech, and high-growth enterprises. This chapter is going to compare Estonian high-growth enterprises from different business fields and technological insensitivity levels.

Estonia is a very small country in Eastern Europe with a history of Soviet occupation. From the Soviet period, there have been several myths and negative attitudes toward entrepreneurship, because entrepreneurship was considered a crime. However, since the independence, several hard reforms have been carried out and Estonia has been considered a success story. Currently, Estonia has been also called the "most advanced digital society in the world." Already in 1997, Estonia established an e-Governance system. This system allows citizens to access many public services online. In 2001, Estonia created the Digital Identity Card, which allows all citizens to access numerous services such as transportation, e-school, banking services, driving licenses, personal medical records, etc. And in 2005, Estonia became the first country in the world to allow citizens to vote online.

This background of a high-tech, digital society with a stable economic environment has made Estonia the Silicon Valley of Eastern Europe. Estonia, with its small and smart society, has become a breeding ground for start-ups. Despite being a small country with only 1.3 million people, the country's tech start-up ecosystem continues to grow, with start-ups raising around 330M EUR in 2018. According to Startup Estonia, we have currently around 650 start-ups in Estonia. Most of them operate in the following sectors: Business Software, Services and Human Resources (HR) (108 start-ups), AdTech and Creative Tech (98 start-ups), FinTech (69 start-ups), HealthTech, Life Sciences and Wellness (58 start-ups), and CleanTech (48 start-ups) (Startup Estonia, 2019). Estonian Tax and Customs Board shows that at the end of the second quarter of 2019 Estonian start-ups employed 4,848 people and employment taxes of 32.7M EUR were paid in the first 6 months of 2019. In the first half of 2019, Estonian start-ups generated 155M EUR in turnover, which is an increase of 3% compared to the same time in 2018. During the first half of 2019, 117M EUR was invested in Estonian start-ups. In total, there have been 24 new investment deals, with an average size of 4.43M EUR per deal. Despite the lower investment amount than the same time period in the previous year, there was a rise in the number of deals made (15 investment deals made within the first 6 months of 2018) (Startup Estonia, 2019).

The problem addressed by the research is how to assure/provide a supportive entrepreneurial ecosystem and encourage growth and innovation. Despite the growth of hi-tech and hi-growth sectors, they also have some barriers and difficulties. Therefore, it is important to understand if there are any differences between mainstream compared to either high-tech or high-growth business models as well as the kind of support required for various business model components and development phases.

The study is based on three Estonian enterprises. Data is retrieved from the Estonian Business Register and other resources (home pages, public interviews with stakeholders, reports, etc.). First, the authors focus on the business model and its components in the case of mainstream, high-tech, and high-growth enterprises. Second, the authors analyzed the components of business models and compared the similarities and differences of the components. And thirdly, the results were discussed and conclusions were made.

This chapter is organized into four sections. The chapter begins with Section 1, which gives an overview of the current state of discourse on a business model, covers and compares the business model components, and indicates differences between high-tech and high-growth enterprises. Section 2 gives an overview of the methodology employed. Section 3 contains an analysis of the case of Estonian enterprises. Finally, Section 4 includes discussions and conclusions and provides an analytical summary of the findings.

4.2 The Concept of Business Model in the Context of Ecosystem

The business model as a theoretical concept has significantly advanced during the last decades. Starting from Schumpeter (1934), the business model concept has developed from mainstream business to e-commerce (Magretta, 2002) and then to modern-day, high-tech, or high-growth start-up models (Osterwalder and Pigneur, 2009).

The business model as a concept has many definitions. One of the simplest definitions is: "The business model is the logic of making money for your business in the current business environment" (Linder and Cantrell, 2001). This definition is based on the classic questions: Who is a customer? and What is valuable to the customer? (Drucker, 1994). Understanding of the business model and market strategy has propagated the need for timeliness of reciprocal matching and development (Zott and Amit, 2008). Going even further, Schweizer (2005) defined the business model along three dimensions: (1) value chain constellation, or how value is created; (2) market power of innovators versus owner of complementary assets, indicating how enterprises create sustainable competitive advantage; and (3) total revenue potential, referring to the revenue model. For a more concise approach, Chesbrough (2010) and Chesbrough and Rosenbloom (2002) suggested that a business model fulfills the following functions:

- Articulates the value proposition (i.e., the value created for users by an offering based on technology).
- Identifies a market segment and specifies the revenue generation mechanism (i.e., users to whom technology is useful and for what purpose).
- Defines the structure of the value chain required to create and distribute the offering and complementary assets needed to support the position in the chain.
- Details the revenue mechanism(s) by which the enterprise will be paid for the offering.
- Estimates the cost structure and profit potential (given value proposition and value chain structure).
- Describes the position of the enterprise within the value network linking suppliers and customers (including identification of potential competitors).
- Formulates the competitive strategy by which the innovating enterprise will gain and hold an advantage over rivals.

Due to its functions, the business model design, itself, has become one of the important innovation processes, which induces further analysis of the business model innovation (Chesbrough, 2003a). However, a suitable business model is a key success factor for changing the innovation (process) (Kelli et al., 2013).

A business networking model guides how a network of enterprises creates value for both the customers and the network by developing a collective understanding of business opportunities and modeling their actions (Palo and Tähtinen, 2013). One form to get gains from the networking model is through the entrepreneurial ecosystem. The function of entrepreneurial ecosystems is not only to create or absorb ideas but also to turn ideas into innovations and commercialize them. The entrepreneurial ecosystem in the context of high-growth enterprises determines "a set of interconnected entrepreneurial actors (both potential and existing), entrepreneurial organizations (e.g., enterprises, venture capitalists, business angels, and banks), institutions (universities, public sector agencies, and financial bodies), and entrepreneurial processes (e.g., the business birth rate, number of high-growth enterprises, levels of 'blockbuster entrepreneurship,' number of serial entrepreneurs, degree of sell-out mentality within enterprises, and levels of entrepreneurial ambition) which formally and informally coalesce to connect, mediate, and govern the performance within the local entrepreneurial environment," (Mason and Brown, 2013). This approach does not take into account traditional entrepreneurship and stated that it is clear that the entrepreneurial ecosystem approach does not, by definition, include the traditional statistical indicators of entrepreneurship, such as "self-employment" or "small businesses," into entrepreneurship (Stam, 2015). Strong sets of social attributes such as networks, mentors, and investment capital within a region help to reinforce and reproduce the ecosystem's pre-existing culture by normalizing these practices and creating new stories of successful entrepreneurship that enter into the region's history (Spiegel, 2017).

4.3 Globalization in the Business Model

Changes in the process of starting of businesses and the fast growth of technology during the last years have led to the evolution of business models. This development has changed the start-up field and has given boosts to knowledge- and technology-based enterprises. Changing the direction of start-ups' products and/or services has also changed knowledge- and technology-based start-up business models. The business model is a concept that can mobilize the technical potential to transform it into a profitable economic business. The business model mediates the relationship between technology and economic value (Chesbrough and Rosenbloom, 2002). Technology, by itself, does not have objective value. The economic value of technology remains latent until it is commercialized in some way via a business model (Chesbrough, 2010).

Technology insensitivity, or in other words hi-tech, is differently defined by many authors. The main characters of hi-tech are connected with the complexity and newness of the product or production process (Steenhuis and De Bruijn, 2006). There are several factors considered when characterizing modern, high-tech business and its environment:

- Complexity and high uncertainty of developmental factors and environment.
- High level of R&D and cooperation between research institutions and enterprises.
- High resource requirements in early product development.
- The need for a highly qualified workforce.
- Interdisciplinary business competence at an early stage of business and product development.
- Entrepreneurial leadership, other social competences, and networking.

To a large extent, these features point to both the open innovation model in high-tech entrepreneurship and the potential barriers that small- and medium-sized enterprises (SMEs) must overcome before the market breakthrough (Kelli et al., 2013). As a result, business model decisions strongly influence and characterize the way new technology-based enterprises operate and the strategy they put in place (Onetti et al., 2012). Not only is the technology intensity of a new enterprise specific to this new era, but also the need to become global is predominant at this time. Knowledge intensity of an enterprise serves as an incentive for internalization and globalization since the expenses of developing new knowledge are virtually the same whether for local, regional, or global markets (Mets and Kelli, 2011). Hi-tech small and medium-sized enterprises (HSMEs) are defined here according to Mets and Kelli's (2011) definition. Therefore, HSMEs are the enterprises which are contributing to the creation of high-technology themselves and not only using cheap labor for assembly operations in their locations.

Going international is often the only way for Estonian enterprises to survive because the Estonian market is very small and limited. The two most widely used concepts of internationalization of enterprises are as follow. First, the "born global" (BG) model is seen when business organizations from or near their founding seek superior international business performance from the application of knowledge-based resources to the sale of outputs in multiple countries (Knight and Cavusgil, 2004). Alternatively, after operating for a long time in the domestic market, a critical incident can lead to globalization in the "born again global" (BAG) model (Mets and Kelli, 2011). Both models point to the need to create the prerequisites for bringing HSMEs into the global market early in the enterprise's development. In a small country context where the local market is limited in resources, both financial and in terms of territorial coverage of intellectual property (IP) protection, enterprises need to find ways to multiply product (service) knowledge across all (target) market segments through their business model to the direction of growth (Mets, 2013).

IP has an important role in the enterprise's business model or the function of supporting technology and market barrier, blocker, and market, and knowledge multiplication in the development of a technology enterprise (Mets, 2013). In high-tech and hi-growth sectors, intellectual property rights (IPR) strategies are developed combining the use of different IP rights. Original know-how must be protected before it is made public and/or marketed. However, it is also necessary to decide at an early stage on whether to enter new markets, as IP protection is governed by both regional and country-specific legislation, yet the novelty requirement for knowledge and other know-how to obtain a patent is generally global. It is important how a small business builds its IP protection. IPR legislation is quite different among the countries, and it can also be a barrier for entering the country's market (Kuźnar and Folfas, 2018). If the IPR legislation is weak, local enterprises have strong incentives to copy or imitate foreign inventions, thus replacing some imports by home production. The legal owners of IPR may refrain from exporting to a market with weak IPR because potential imitators can diminish the profitability of the enterprise's activity in that market. However, the high level of protection of IPR could also prevent trade since foreign exporting enterprises are granted exclusive rights to products and technologies in the importing country. The rights-holding exporters benefit from the monopolistic power and decrease exports in return for higher prices and profits (Kuźnar and Folfas, 2018). The ability to replicate the business model across new markets requires a business model form to which barriers to these markets are easier to overcome than the competitor's environment. IP can support entry into new markets and ensure freedom of action in a specific market as well as act as a barrier to competitors.

The success of technology enterprises is ultimately determined by technological competencies (knowledge) and market replication capabilities, that is, business model replication capabilities.

The market potential of IP combined with the technological and business model replication capability is a prerequisite. One of the key factors is finding HSMEs investors and providing venture capital funding into a growth enterprise for a technology enterprise.

Today's technological advances, where IT tools have become business tools of the day, are pushing for success factors that are harder to copy. It has also meant increasing the share of R&D and IP, including new knowledge, in the corporate value chain. Licensing technology is an important part of managing IP (Chesbrough, 2003b). There is a growing awareness of the need to protect IP, as it is based on innovative solutions and has led to an increase in the number of registered inventions. Investors have increasingly begun to observe the existence and protection of intellectual omnipotence, and the number of patented technical solutions has begun to be seen as an indicator of innovation both at the enterprise level and nationally (Mets, 2013). The IP value relates to the present value of the product (see financial methods). It includes three types of IP: technical (patent utility, software functionality – copyright, trade secret), reputation (trademark, brand name, etc.), and process (business methods and ownership of business processes) (Camino and Manenti, 2015). In Europe, software is protected by copyright while it is not patentable "as such." High-tech IP in Europe is mostly protected by trademark and software copyright, but US patenting is also used. Trademarks are considered as outcomes of establishing recognizable designations and symbols for goods and services, as well as enterprises' identities (Mendonca et al., 2004). In the information and communication technology (ICT) sector, different innovation models and practices coexist. This coexistence has probably become most evident in the software industry. Developers use patents more and more to protect their products (Kuźnar and Folfas, 2018). At the same time, open-source software (OSS) is making inroads into several segments of the industry. In the last 20 years, discussions about the role of IPRs in software have also been fueled by the success of OSS. Based on an alternative way to protect innovation known as "copy left," OSS calls into question the traditional role of IPRs as mechanisms to promote computer program innovation. Besides, enterprises often adopt hybrid business models combining open and proprietary approaches in software development and distribution (Camino and Manenti, 2015). However, as we detail below, embedded software, or computer-implemented inventions in technical jargon, can be patented.

4.4 Components of the Business Model Design

The business model consists of different components which illustrate how the business model works. Investigation of the components of a business model is valuable in terms of translating business plans into business processes (Osterwalder and Pigneur, 2009). A business model articulates the logic and provides data and other evidence that demonstrates how a business creates and delivers value to customers. It also outlines the architecture of revenue, cost, and profit associated with the business enterprise delivering that value (Teece, 2010). In this chapter, the authors observe three business model concepts and their division into components.

According to Teece (2010), components of the business model design are (1) selecting the technologies and features to be embedded in the product/service; (2) determining the benefit to the customer from consuming/using the product/service; (3) identifying market segments to be targeted; (4) confirming available revenue streams; (5) and (6) designing mechanisms to capture value. The whole process aims to create value for customers, entice payments, and convert payments to profit.

Morris et al. (2005, 2006) proposed a framework for business model components. Each of the six components is evaluated on three levels. At the foundation level, the model is defined in terms of a standardized set of decisions that can be quantified. A benefit of this standardization is the ability to make comparisons across models from a broad universe of ventures. At the proprietary level, considerable scope for innovation exists within each model component. The model becomes a form of IP, with some entrepreneurs obtaining patents for their models.

Morris et al. (2005) built their framework on six key questions:

- How will the enterprise create value (value proposition)?
- For whom will the enterprise create value (market)?
- What is the enterprise's internal source of advantage (internal processes)?
- How will the enterprise position itself in the marketplace (economic model)?
- How will the enterprise make money (competitive strategy)?
- What is the entrepreneur's time, scope, and size ambitions (personal/investor factors)?

In the Morris et al. (2005) framework, all the six components are evaluated at three levels. At the foundation level, the model is defined in terms of a standardized set of decisions that can be quantified. At the proprietary level, considerable scope for innovation exists within each model component. The model becomes a form of IP, with some entrepreneurs obtaining patents for their models. And at the third level, the rules provide a clearer sense of the enterprise's value proposition and are a source of guidance regarding actions that might compromise the value equation.

Watson (2006) described the business model as the enterprise's operations, including all its components, functions, and processes that determine the cost for itself and the value for the client.

The business model is demonstrated through six components, namely, competitors, customers, economy, management, products, and suppliers (Table 4.1).

In the case of Watson's (2006) business model concept, it has a complex and in-depth nature. The most important component is the sector-based analysis of what is usually considered as a part of the environment of business model. This concept allows us to look at

Table 4.1 Structure of Business Model Components

WATSON (2006)	MORRIS ET AL. (2005)	CHESBROUGH (2003, 2006)	OSTERWALDER AND PIGNEUR (2009)
Products	Value proposition	Value proposition	Value proposition
Competitors	Market	Market segments	Customer segment
Economy	Economic model	Cost structure	Cost structure
Management		Profit potential	Key activities
Customers	Internal processes	Value network	Customer relationships
Suppliers	Competitive strategy	Competitive strategy	Key resources
		Value chain	Key partnerships
	Personal/investor factors		Channels
			Revenue streams

high-tech start-ups at the sectoral level and understand better how the entrepreneurial ecosystem supports new enterprises.

Chesbrough (2003, 2006) divides business model components into six categories: value proposition, market segment, value chain, costs structure and profit potential, value network (in other words also entrepreneurial ecosystem), and competitive strategy. In a more explained matter, these six functions are the following:

- Articulate the value proposition – that is, the value created for users by offering.
- Identify a market segment – that is, the users to whom the offering and its purpose are useful.
- Define the structure of the value chain required by the enterprise to create and distribute the offering, and determine the complementary assets needed to support the enterprise's position in this chain (this includes the enterprise's suppliers and customers and should extend from raw materials to the final customer).
- Specify the revenue generation mechanisms for the enterprise, and estimate the cost structure and profit potential of producing the offering, given the value proposition and value-chain structure chosen.
- Describe the position of the enterprise within the value network, linking suppliers and customers, including identification of potential competitors.
- Formulate the competitive strategy by which the innovating enterprise will gain and hold an advantage over rivals.

In the field of start-ups, the most commonly used solutions to demonstrate the business model of the enterprise are a one-page business plan or business model canvas by Osterwalder and Pigneur (2009). They define the business model using nine components: customer segments, value propositions, channels, customer relationships, revenue streams, key resources, key activities, key partners, and cost structure. The use of the business model increased greatly due to technological advances and the rise of Internet businesses in the 2000s. Technology also plays an important role in defining a business model. Creating new business models is a business activity that requires both a technological and a market position view. The business model is focused on a tool that lies between the technological development of the enterprise and the generation of economic returns. The business model provides a framework that leverages technological features and capabilities as input to make them economically viable through customers and markets (Chesbrough and Rosenbloom, 2002).

Customer segments are defined by five types of markets: mass, niche, segmented, diversified, and multi-sided markets. The mass market focuses on one large group of customers with broadly similar needs and problems. The niche market has tailored products to specific requirements. Segmented markets have slightly different needs and problems. Diversified market segments serve two unrelated customer segments with very different needs and problems. Multi-sided markets serve two or more independent customer segments.

Value propositions create value for a customer segment through a distinct mix of elements catering to that segment's needs. Values may be quantitative (e.g., price or speed of service) or qualitative (e.g., design or customer experience). Various elements include newness, performance, price, risk reduction, customization, etc.

Channels' building block describes how an enterprise communicates with and reaches its customer segments to deliver the value proposition. Channels have five distinctive phases: (1) awareness – raising awareness among customers about an enterprise's products and services; (2) evaluation – helping customers evaluate an enterprise value proposition; (3) purchase – allowing customers to purchase specific products and services; (4) delivery – delivering a value proposition to customers; and (5) after-sales – providing post-purchase customer support.

Customer relationship building blocks describe the types of relationships an enterprise establishes with specific customer segments.

Customer relationships may be driven by customer acquisition, customer retention, or boosting sales (upselling).

Revenue streams represent the cash an enterprise generates from each customer segment (costs must be subtracted from revenues to create earnings). There are several ways to generate a revenue stream. Asset sales derive from selling ownership rights to a physical product. The usage fee is generated by the use of a particular service. Subscription fees are generated by selling continuous access to service. Lending, renting, or leasing are created by temporarily granting someone the exclusive right to use a particular asset for a fixed period in return for a fee. The brokerage fees derive from intermediation services performed on behalf of two or more parties. The advertising results from fees for advertising a particular product, service, or brand.

Key resources describe the most important assets required to make a business model work. These resources allow an enterprise to create and offer a value proposition, reach markets, maintain relationships with customer segments, and earn revenues. Resources can be physical, intellectual, human, and financial.

Key activities describe the most important things an enterprise must do to make its business model work. Key activities are required to create and offer a value proposition, reach markets, maintain customer relationships, and earn revenues. Key activities differ depending on the business model type.

Key partnerships describe the network of suppliers and partners that makes the business model work. There are four different types of partnerships: (1) strategic alliances between non-competitors; (2) cooperation – strategic partnerships between competitors; (3) joint ventures to develop new enterprises; and (4) buyer-supplier relationships to assure reliable supplies.

Cost structure describes all costs incurred to operate a business model. It is useful to distinguish between two broad classes of the business model cost structure: cost-driven and value-driven. A cost-driven business model focuses on minimizing costs wherever possible. This approach aims at creating and maintaining the leanest possible cost structure, using low price value propositions, maximum automation, and extensive outsourcing. A value-driven business model focuses on value creation. Premium value propositions and a high degree of personalized service usually characterize a value-driven business model.

For this chapter, the authors use the business model components which are developed by Osterwalder and Pigneur (2009) and take the best from other authors.

4.5 Empirical Research

This study's design was guided by our aim to conceptualize the differences between a variety of business models and its elements and bring out differences between mainstream, high-tech, and high-growth enterprises. We focus on high-tech and high-growth enterprise business model components to compare and analyze how the business model components are displayed in the enterprises' actions.

The empirical part of this chapter uses qualitative methods, more specifically, a case study as a research approach. The qualitative method allows deeper and more complex study of the whole phenomena of high-tech and high-growth enterprise growth and globalization. The qualitative method provides information by analyzing and interpreting data. According to this method, social actions are considered as a holistic, interactive, and complicated system, not independent discrete variables, which, as such, may be measured statistically (Rossmann and Rallis, 1998). According to Yin (2003), "case studies are the preferred strategy when 'how' or 'why' questions are being posed, when the investigator has little control over events, and when the focus is on a contemporary phenomenon within some real-life context." These presumptions are applied also within the current study for exploring practices of business model components in high-tech and high-growth enterprises in Estonia. The main characteristic of case studies is the focus on the case and exploring its main factors (Stake, 1995). This is scientifically fruitful, especially for studying business model components, since these practices are influenced by several factors (people and their experiences, local and global practices, technology, IP and interpretations). In our case, we search for answers as to how different business model components can influence the development of enterprise and also what components are important for globalization in the case of high-tech and high-growth cases.

Case studies based on secondary data and personal interviews were used for mapping the main components of the business model (as shown in Table 4.2). Next, webpages and annual reports of the

Table 4.2   Business Model Canvas of A. Le Coq Ltd., Cleveron Ltd., and Pipedrive Ltd.

OSTERWALDER BUSINESS MODEL'S COMPONENTS	A. LE COQ LTD.	CLEVERON LTD.	PIPEDRIVE LTD.
Customer segments	Mass market: • Business customers (restaurants, pubs, etc.)	Niche market: • Business customers (retailer and logistics sector)	Niche market: • Business customers in the sales field
Value propositions	• Old and distinguished brand • Producing and selling beverages (beers, ciders, lemonades, water) • Cooperation with businesses (restaurants, pubs, retailers, etc.) • Lower price • Products are easily accessible • Products are meant for everybody (low customization) • Convenient to use, low differentiation (different taste, same package)	• Well-known brand • Producing and selling smart lockers, parcel robots, and parcel software • Cooperation with retailers and logistics sectors (Walmart, Asda, Inditex, etc.) • Product feature dependent price • Products are specially developed in customer basis • Products are sector-based with high customization • Convenience is highly developed and considered as a main value feature • Global innovation leader in producing robotic parcel terminals	• Well-known brand • Customer relationship management (CRM) tool for salespeople • A unique artificial intelligence-based assistant • Cooperation with retailers and sales enterprises • Subscription fees • Products are developed for specific customer segment (salespeople) • Product is sector-based with high customization • Convenience is highly developed and considered as a main value feature
Channels	• Physical channels (production and logistic departments) • Marketing in social media, television, direct offers for businesses, etc.	• Physical channels (production units and logistics department) • Marketing in the home page, messes, direct offers for businesses, etc.	• Physical channels: offices in the 8 cities (6 countries) • Marketing in the home page, direct offers for businesses, etc.

(*Continued*)

Table 4.2 *(Continued)*   Business Model Canvas of A. Le Coq Ltd., Cleveron Ltd., and Pipedrive Ltd.

OSTERWALDER BUSINESS MODEL'S COMPONENTS	A. LE COQ LTD.	CLEVERON LTD.	PIPEDRIVE LTD.
Customer relationships	• Boosting sales (upselling) • Personal assistance (businesses) • Automated services with private and business customer segments)	• Customer retention • (Dedicated) personal assistance to business customers • Self-service for end-customer (private and business)	• Customer retention • Personalized offers to businesses • Self-service for end-customer
Revenue streams	• Transaction revenues resulting from one-time customer payments • Selling products to retailers • Price (list price or volume dependent)	• Recurring revenues resulting from ongoing payment for maintenance of software • Products • Licensing software • Software • Credits	• Recurring revenues resulting from ongoing payments to provide post-purchase customer support • Subscription fees • Licensing software • Credits
Key resources	• Brand (trademark protected) • IP-based beverages • Customer databases (customers as business clients) • Well-trained sales and production employees	• Brand (trademark protected) • Know-how and IP • Customer databases (customers as businesses and consumers) • Highly trained developers, engineers, sales persons • IT infrastructure • Software • Customer applications	• Brand (trademark protected) • Know-how is protected by business secret, copyright • Customer databases (customers as businesses and customers as end-customers (of businesses) • Highly trained developers, ICT specialist, programmers, salespeople • IT infrastructure

Table 4.2 _(Continued)_   Business Model Canvas of A. Le Coq Ltd., Cleveron Ltd., and Pipedrive Ltd.

OSTERWALDER BUSINESS MODEL'S COMPONENTS	A. LE COQ LTD.	CLEVERON LTD.	PIPEDRIVE LTD.
Key activities	• R&D • Production of beverages • Design and branding • Marketing • Sales	• R&D • Production of package robots • Software development • Platform development • Design and branding • Marketing • Sales • Finding buildings and enterprises, who would need logistic solutions	• R&D • Software development • Platform development • Design and branding • Marketing • Sales • Billing • Legal • Maintenance
Key partnerships	• Olvi Group (mother enterprise), sharing suppliers and products • Subcontractors (some smaller product lines) • Raw material providers • Pubs, restaurants, and other shops as key partners	• Logistic enterprises • Raw material providers • Retail and logistics enterprises • Subcontractor	• Investors • Professional salespeople and/or enterprises
Cost structure	Cost-driven business model: • Producing beverages (fixed and variable costs, production volume dependent)	Value-driven business model: • Personalized services (later maintenance of package robots, etc.) • Selling software, renting storage room in package robots, etc.	Value-driven business model: • Personalized services (after-sales consultations, usage of artificial assistant, etc.); • Licensing fees

enterprises were studied. The data collected was evaluated in the context of business model components; aspects not covered previously and newer trends were mapped; some interpretations were cross-checked.

The comparative analysis of mainstream, high-tech, and high-growth enterprises is based on official business statistics. The purpose of this viewpoint is to clarify how high-tech and high-growth enterprises differ and the potential advantages they possess.

The main criteria for selection of a case study enterprise were the following:

- Estonian origin of the enterprise or/and tight relations with Estonia.
- The enterprise should be a success story, that is, it should have a working business model for global success.
- The main development track of the enterprise should be examined.
- In the case of HSMEs, the main knowledge or/and technology is created in Estonia.
- In the case of HSMEs, the enterprises represent technologies of different fields.

There were several new Estonian enterprises which met the described requirements. We choose three cases that are the best practices in their field and describe most clearly the business model components. These enterprises are Cleveron Ltd. (high-tech), Pipedrive Ltd. (high-growth), and A. Le Coq Ltd. (a classical mainstream enterprise).

Cleveron Ltd., in the present form, was established in 2007. The story behind this is longer. Arno Kütt, one of the owners of Cleveron Ltd., founded Eerung Ltd. in 1993, specializing in the manufacturing and sale of furniture. In 2000, he developed the leading online furniture store, ON24, in Estonia and Finland. In 2006, the logistics department of ON24 was opened for improved delivery of goods, including the development of the parcel terminal hardware and software and its parcel terminal network. As a result, a new enterprise was registered in 2007 under the legal name of Cleveron Ltd., but, initially, it was called SmartPOST. Therefore, Cleveron Ltd. is a typical born global again enterprise. In 2009, a successful Estonian-wide parcel terminal network was opened, which in 2010 was sold with the right to use the SmartPOST name to the Finnish enterprise Itella Corporation. As a result, the name Cleveron Ltd. was used. Cleveron Ltd. founders are Arno Kütt and Peep Kuld, and later on a third member, Indrek Oolup, joined. In 2015, the share capital was increased, after which private limited enterprise was transformed into the joint-stock enterprise. Currently, Cleveron has four stockholders

(Tera Ventures, Bagira Ltd., Parem Mööel Ltd., and Sibo Invest Ltd.). The enterprise's core business has changed over the years and, since 2014, is manufacturing general-purpose machinery (NACE code 28.29). Cleveron Ltd. is a pioneer in the field as a provider of new solutions. Cleveron Ltd. offers a complete solution that includes hardware, software, and after-sales service based on customer needs and package size. The main products are automation-based SnapLocker and CleverBox as well as robotics-based 5-meter tower PackRobot, which accommodates up to 500 parcels and CleverFlex Ltd. Today the factory in Viljandi produces about 4–5 PackRobots per day; this number should at least double within the next year. Cleveron Ltd. is the global innovation leader in robotic parcel terminals and last-mile click and collect solutions for the retail and logistics sectors.

Pipedrive Ltd. is a software enterprise engaged in the development, marketing, and customer support of sales management software Pipedrive Ltd. (NACE code 62.01). Pipedrive Ltd. was founded in 2010 by five Estonians, namely Timo Rein, Urmas Purde, Martin Henk, Ragnar Sass, and Martin Tajur. Pipedrive Ltd. is a classic example of a born global enterprise – it was founded to solve the global problem with a global extent. Pipedrive Ltd. has gained over 90 million USD in funding, and this has also changed the ownership structure in the enterprise. Investors include venture capital enterprises Bessemer Venture Partners, Paua Ventures, Rembrandt Venture Partners, AngelPad, Storm Ventures, and TMT Investments as well as angel investors like David Hinrikus and Andy McLoughlin. The enterprise has offices in Tallinn and Tartu (Estonia), New York and Florida (USA), Lisbon (Portugal), London (United Kingdom), Prague (Czech Republic), and Dublin (Ireland). By the end of 2019, the enterprise had users in more than 170 countries, with the largest markets in the United States, Brazil, England, Canada, Australia, and France. In 2019, Pipedrive Ltd. launched a new generation of software, with a unique artificial intelligence-based assistant that will advise salespeople on the most appropriate next step for a successful customer transaction.

Pipedrive Ltd. is one of the fastest-growing enterprises in Europe by the Financial Times, one of the best enterprises for women to work for according to Inc. Magazine, and best employer in the Private Sector 2016–2019 by Estonia's Dream Employer.

A. Le Coq Ltd. was founded in 1807 and is the most prominent drink manufacturer in Estonia. In 1997, the Finnish brewery Olvi Oyj acquired shares of Tartu Õlletehas (Tartu Brewery), and a year later the holding enterprise A. Le Coq Ltd. was founded. Therefore, from globalization viewpoint, A. Le Coq Ltd. is a BAG enterprise. In 1999, the Finnish holding enterprise decided to completely renovate the brewery in Tartu. Substantial investments by Olvi Plc. (new fermenting cellar, boiling unit, bottling line, filter, and new storage facilities) turned Tartu Õlletehas Ltd. into an enterprise with up-to-date equipment that was the most modern one in the Baltic region at the time. Top-quality production facilities made it possible to set higher marketing and sales goals. In 2007, the enterprise celebrated its 200th anniversary. In 2007, the enterprise name, A. Le Coq Tartu Brewery, was shortened into A. Le Coq Ltd., which was previously used from 1913 until 1940. Olvi's subsidiary Ltd., in the same year, A. Le Coq acquired the entire stock of the Estonian enterprise Finelin Ltd. Since 2009, A. Le Coq's Ltd. mother enterprise has been Olvi OYJ. A. Le Coq' Ltd. product portfolio includes 11 different product groups. The main product group is beer, followed by juice, water, and soft drinks, and the remaining product groups such as cider, light alcoholic beverages, active juice drinks, sports and energy drinks, syrups, and kvass. A. Le Coq Ltd. holds the leading position in the Estonian beverage market in the categories of beer, juice, and long drinks and ranks a strong second in the production of water, soft drinks, and cider.

A. Le Coq Ltd. has been awarded the title of the most competitive enterprise of the Estonian food industry for 11 years in a row, which is the result of the enterprise's constant commitment to product quality and product development. The enterprise has already invested 73M EUR in production and product development, which has made it one of the most modern drink industries in the Baltic States.

4.6 Main Findings and Discussion

This section gives an overview of the main findings and differences between mainstream, high-growth, and high-tech enterprises' business model compounds. According to the business model and main activity, enterprises are divided into mainstream (A. Le Coq Ltd.), high-tech, (Cleveron Ltd.), and high-growth (Pipedrive Ltd.) segments.

Customer segments component is defining the different groups of people or organizations that an enterprise aims to reach and serve (Osterwalder and Pigneur, 2009). The main findings are that in the case of comparing mainstream, high-growth, and high-tech enterprises, the customer segments types are different. A. Le Coq's Ltd. business model is focused on the mass market and does not distinguish between different customer segments. The enterprise sells mainly to business customers and its product end-users are also private customers. At the same time, the high-growth enterprise, Pipedrive Ltd., and high-tech enterprise, Cleveron Ltd., are focusing on a niche market and cater to specific, specialized customer segments. Pipedrive is focused on the business customers in the field of sales, and Cleveron Ltd. is focused on business customers in the field of package robots.

The value proposition is the reason why customers turn to one enterprise over another (Osterwalder and Pigneur, 2009). In the case of A. Le Coq Ltd., Cleveron Ltd., and Pipedrive Ltd., they all are well-known brands. Also, the brand name is protected in every case. All the enterprises value the newness but in their different levels. A. Le Coq Ltd., as a mainstream enterprise, focuses on developing new tastes and combinations of beverages. Both Cleveron Ltd., as a high-tech enterprise, and Pipedrive Ltd., as a high-growth enterprise, are the innovation leaders in their respective fields. In the case of the mainstream example, the price of the product is lower, but high-tech and high-growth examples' prices are product feature dependent on price or subscription fees. Products' customization is also different: Mainstream enterprises' products are meant for everybody with low customization, but high-tech and high-growth enterprises' products are sector-based with high customization or developed especially for a specific customer segment. Convenience and usability are the third issues. In the case of A. Le Coq Ltd., convenience is an important and specific solution in canning, distribution, and availability. But this isn't the main component of the enterprise's value proposition. In the case of Cleveron Ltd. and Pipedrive Ltd., convenience is highly developed and considered as a main value proposition feature.

Channels component describes how an enterprise communicates with and reaches its customers' segments to deliver value proposition (Osterwalder and Pigneur, 2009). At the same time, it is crucial to find the right mix of channels to satisfy the way how customers want to be reached. Some differences are in the channel types like direct (salesforce, web sales) or indirect (own stores, partner stores, or wholesalers). For example, high-tech and high-growth enterprises tend to use direct channels for sales. Cleveron Ltd. is selling its package robots directly to big retail and logistics enterprises; information about the products is available on the Internet (homepage, newspaper articles, etc.). Pipedrive Ltd. offers its software through direct offers or webpage. The more traditional enterprise, A. Le Coq Ltd., uses more indirect channels like wholesalers, partner restaurants, and pubs. The same conclusion can be made about after-sales support – high-tech and high-growth enterprises, whose products are meant for a niche market, are paying more attention and provide direct post-purchase support for their customers.

Cost structure is one of the most important parts of the business model. In the comparison of mainstream, high-tech, and high-growth enterprises, it occurs that high-tech and high-growth tend to be value-driven, not cost-driven. A. Le Coq Ltd. cost structure is cost-driven, competing with other similar products in the market by price, and characterized with fixed costs (salaries, R&D, maintenance costs, rent, physical manufacturing facilities) and variable costs (raw material, logistics costs, taxes, etc.). Cleveron Ltd. and Pipedrive Ltd. business models are value-driven. Although they have fixed and variable costs, they are selling the unique value of their products or services.

Key activities component describes the most important things an enterprise must do to make its business model work. The main key activities are similar, like marketing, sales, branding, and R&D. All investigated enterprises valued their research and development input and presented this part as one of the most important Key Activities. Differences appeared in the production, where aside physical product versus software, there were differences in high-tech–based production like Cleveron's Ltd. robots or Pipedrive's Ltd. software versus knowledge-based production of beverages.

Customer relationships component describes the types of relationships an enterprise establishes with specific customer segments (Osterwalder and Pigneur, 2009). Customer relationships are driven by different motivations. A. Le Coq's Ltd. business model is driven by boosting sales (upselling), offering big discounts to new products or seasonable beverages. Enterprises like Cleveron Ltd. and Pipedrive

Ltd. are driven by customer retention, focusing on the customer and its needs. Enterprises' relationships with particular customer segments are also different. In the case of all enterprises, there are business customers (direct) and private customers (indirect). For business customers, personal assistance is offered. In the case of technology-intensive enterprises like Pipedrive Ltd., more technological solutions are used (e.g., an artificial assistant). In the case of the Osterwalder and Pigneur business model canvas, the customer relationships and segments box do not allow to show the whole complexity between these business-to-business cases. For example, in the case of Cleveron Ltd., the customer is the retail enterprise, but the consumers are private persons/other enterprises. The same logic applies also in the case of A. Le Coq Ltd. (customer is a pub, a restaurant, a shop; consumers are private persons) and Pipedrive Ltd. (customer is a sales enterprise; consumers are salespersons). In the case of private consumers, automated services like feedback via emails, social media, or phone are offered.

Key resources are the assets required to make a business model work and can be categorized into physical, intellectual, human, and financial resources (Osterwalder and Pigneur, 2009).

Physical resources are represented in all three cases. A. Le Coq Ltd. and Cleveron Ltd., as production enterprises, have factories, other buildings, and logistics departments. Pipedrive Ltd. has physical offices in eight cities in six different countries.

Intellectual resources such as trademarks, patents, and copyrights are used. All three enterprises have protected their IP, using different strategies. Pipedrive Ltd. is a software enterprise focusing on developing marketing and customer support sales management software. Using IP protection in software, we must understand the characteristics of the software production: (1) cumulativeness of the innovation process (Innovation in the software industry is highly cumulative and a common practice in the development of new computer programs is code re-use.); (2) short product life-cycles (As a matter of fact, most programs become obsolete in only a few years and are quickly replaced by new applications.); and (3) high level of abstraction (Software algorithms can be represented in several different ways; at the same time, two apparently different algorithms may turn out to be equivalent).

Pipedrive Ltd. has chosen to protect their IP mainly with trademark and copyright, but they also use other possibilities. The Pipedrive

Services (the web site, system, content, platform, and all content, services, and/or products available on or through the Platform), Pipedrive Materials (the visual interfaces, graphics, design, systems, methods, information, computer code, software, services, "look and feel," organization, compilation of the content, code, data, and all other elements of the Pipedrive Ltd. Services), Pipedrive Ltd. trade names and trademarks, and any parts or elements thereof are solely and exclusively owned and operated by the supplier and its third-party vendors and hosting partners. Pipedrive Materials are protected by copyright, trade dress, patent, trade secrets, and trademark laws, international conventions and treaties, and all other relevant IP and proprietary rights laws. The research (Blind, 2007) finds out that the most common mechanisms used to protect software innovation were internal confidentiality (secrecy agreements with employees), lead time, and customer relations management. All these factors are also in the focus of Pipedrive Ltd. activities.

A. Le Coq Ltd. has a long history and traditions. For the enterprise, it is very important to have a strong trademark. A. Le Coq Ltd. is one of the most prestigious brands in Estonia. A. Le Coq Ltd. has also seven registered industrial designs. In addition to industrial design solutions, the enterprise also has its IP in the field of technologies – in 2010, the enterprise adopted a technology unique to beer production in Estonia. To maintain their market position, they have also acquired other enterprises' IP-based beverages – for example, in the spring of 2010, the colas segment was added to the soft drinks' product group, and A. Le Coq Ltd. began producing Royal Crown Cola, an American cola drink.

High-tech enterprise Cleveron's Ltd. strategy is to protect all new products by IP rights to ensure the client that they are purchasing the original product. Cleveron Ltd. registered its trademark first in the European Union (EU) in 2010. It was also their first registration with the European Union Intellectual Property Office (EUIPO). A registered trademark ensures that Cleveron's Ltd. innovative products are appropriately protected – a factor, which has become increasingly important as Cleveron Ltd. continues to enter new markets around the world. Nowadays, their IP portfolio has grown rapidly: They have filed over 100 applications in more than ten countries. They combine various IP rights, including but not limited to copyrights, patents, utility models, design solutions, trademarks, and service marks. The main IP protection rights include patents on smart locks, modular parcel terminal for sending parcels, self-service parcel terminal with optimized shelving arrangement, method for increasing the speed of discharge and insertion of postal objects in a parcel terminal.

Cleveron Ltd. has also had some problems with patents – some enterprises have tried to steal their IP and create their products with their know-how. Board members Arno Kütt and Peep Kuld say that design cannot be protected in China. According to Chinese legislation, a copier can only be prosecuted when he or she admits to having copied a product. They also learned their lesson in Russia. It is there that Cleveron Ltd. used to have one of its first paying customers, who bought over a 100 parcel terminals. The collaboration ended with the Russians dismantling the machine and copying it.

HR is required in every enterprise, but people are particularly prominent in certain business models (Osterwalder and Pigneur, 2009). The importance of the quality of HR is dependent on the field of activity. For example, in high-tech and high-growth enterprises like Cleveron Ltd. and Pipedrive Ltd., experienced and highly trained experts are extremely important. For this purpose, Cleveron Ltd. established in cooperation with Estonian Entrepreneurship University of Applied Sciences (EUAS) a Cleveron Academy with curricula Robotic Software Development, where specialized employees are trained for developing robotic solutions. This initiative served two purposes. First, it enables them to educate specialized specialists for the enterprise; and second, it enables us to give something back to the entrepreneurial ecosystem. Also, high-tech and high-growth enterprises are supporting intrapreneurship, that is, entrepreneurship inside the enterprise.

Key partnerships component describes enterprise's key partners, suppliers, and the resources that are acquired from partners, and the key activities partners do perform for enterprise (Osterwalder and Pigneur, 2009). All investigated enterprises have some similarities and some differences in this regard. Producing enterprises like A. Le Coq Ltd. and Cleveron Ltd. need raw material providers and subcontractors for smaller parts. In this case, it is buyer-supplier relationships to assure reliable supplies. An important part of the key partnerships is financial partners. For example, A. Le Coq Ltd. gains its investments from the mother enterprise, Pipedrive Ltd. from risk investors, and Cleveron Ltd. has gained some money from EU structural funds.

An important part of a business model is financial planning to find new applications for existing resources or to save costs and thereby generate additional revenue. Financial planning is closely intertwined with all areas of the enterprise on a day-to-day basis, allowing the enterprise management to agree on a strategy, set measurable goals, accountability, and plan for change. Revenue streams represent the cash an enterprise generates from each Customer Segment.

Table 4.3 shows a brief overview of enterprises' economic performance.

Cleveron Ltd. has received several grants from EU support mechanisms in 2013–2018, and this support has been very important for developing innovative solutions. In 2018, the sales revenue

Table 4.3 Overview of Revenue Streams and Main Costs (thousands EUR)

	2013	2014	2015	2016	2017	2018
CLEVERON LTD.						
Sales revenue	3,980	4,219	2,511	32,578	11,222	47,686
Investments	596	13,459	802	1,356	1,893	5,825
EU Grants	346	85	50	0	80	277
Intangible assets	836	986	1,585	2,025,707	3,146	3,964
Labor costs	811	1,028	1,168	1,509,212	2,819	6,213
EBIT	1,519	1,110	88	−201,502	783	7,569
Net income	1,452	1,009	108	−212,547	724	7,622
PIPEDRIVE LTD.						
Sales revenue	818	2,171	4,976	10,255	20,108	31,812
Investments	421	647	1,335	2,044	2,907	5,504
Intangible assets	594	1,064	1,838	2,969	4,566	6,288
Labor Costs	793	1,649	3,346	7,101	10,966	14,831
EBIT	−371	−520	−1,787	−3,063	−376	−1,551
Net Income	−380	−555	−1846	−3101	−479	−1,504
A. LE COQ LTD.						
Sales revenue	81,259	81,962	77,100	76,926	73,948	70,377
Investments	5,463	5,942	5,691	7,012	10,985	2,259
Intangible assets	386	253	129	242	255	211
Labor costs	6,929	7,813	8,045	8,310	8,584	8,307
EBIT	15,999	16,504	15,913	15,388	14,740	14,011
Net income	13,888	14,533	14,055	13,567	12,855	12,272

increased 4.2 times (325%) to 47,685,524 EUR, which is higher than the total sales revenue for the previous ten years. The average number of employees in 2018 was 142 (2017: 87), an increase of 63% over the year. The enterprise invested a total of 5,825,178 EUR in 2018. Of this, 3,555,000 EUR was financed from own resources for the extension of the development and production building from 3,000 m^2 to 10,500 m^2. Today over 3,000 machines are installed, and their parcel lockers and robots can be found in over 20 countries worldwide.

The Pipedrive Ltd. team has also grown steadily over the period 2013–2018 – from 18 in 2013 to 288 in 2018. Over the same period, labor costs have increased by as much as 95%. Cash flows from investing activities have increased by 92% during 2013–2018. The enterprise's operating loss has only increased over the period 2013–2018, amounting to –1,551,544 EUR in 2018. Pipedrive has gained more than 90 million dollars of funding from investors.

Comparing the A. Le Coq Ltd. sales revenue for the period 2013–2018, it appears that sales revenue decreased by 15%, including export to the EU countries by 18%. The economic performance of 2017 and 2018 was strongly influenced by the doubling of excise duty rates on beer and low-alcohol beverages, which led to a decline in domestic sales of these products. The average number of employees has both increased and decreased over the years – 311 in 2013 and 305 in 2018. At the same time, labor costs have increased by 18% between 2013 and 2018. Cash flow from investing activities for the period 2013–2018 decreased by –142%.

All in all, Cleveron Ltd. and Pipedrive Ltd. have grown over 90% in revenue over the period 2013–2018 and will continue to capture new markets. While sales of A. Le Coq Ltd. products have fallen by –15%, exports to non-EU countries have increased by as much as 82%. The same trend is observed for investments – both Cleveron Ltd. and Pipedrive Ltd. have attracted over 90% over the same period, but A. Le Coq's Ltd. investments have declined (–142%). Cleveron Ltd. has also successfully applied for EU funding, and its business model analysis shows that it has probably been made possible by knowledge-based production. The business model shows that Pipedrive's Ltd. investments are related to venture capitalists, and A. Le Coq's Ltd. investments are originated from parent enterprise Olvi.

4.7 Conclusion

The literature review revealed different concepts of business models and their components. Some of them are more suitable for business as usual or in other words mainstream enterprises like Watson (2006); some of them are technology-based like Teece (2010) or Osterwalder and Pigneur (2009), some of them value networking like Chesbrough (2003, 2006) or protecting IP like Morris et al. (2005). For conducting this research, the business model concept and components of Osterwalder and Pigneur (2009) was selected. Comparison of three business models and their components in the case of the high-growth, high-tech, and mainstream enterprises revealed some differences.

First, enterprises with different globalization initiatives were included. Two of them, high-tech enterprise Cleveron Ltd. and mainstream enterprise A. Le Coq Ltd. are BAG enterprises, which operated for a long time in the domestic market and then internationalize. The high-growth enterprise Pipedrive Ltd. is a classic example of a BG enterprise. BG and BAG enterprises need different focuses on entrepreneurial ecosystems.

The protection of IP is critically important for knowledge-based enterprises. All three enterprises are protecting their IPs. For all enterprises, the trademark protection is very important. For the high-tech enterprise, the main issue is how to patent their creations and solutions; and high-growth software enterprise is using more copyright possibilities for all their services and materials. Therefore, knowledge-based enterprises need help from the entrepreneurial ecosystem.

Investigation of revenue streams revealed that high-tech production enterprises gained investments from public funds (EU structural funds); riskier high-growth enterprises gain money from investors or business angels, and traditional production enterprises' investments come from the parent enterprise. It is easily explainable with the newness and innovativeness of knowledge-based products in the case of Cleveron Ltd.

The study is not free from limitations. First, the study is based on Estonian enterprises only. It is necessary to validate the results in other countries, which is a potential avenue for further research. Second, in the case of customer relationships and segment components, the Osterwalder and Pigneur business model canvas does not allow to show the whole complexity between these business-to-business cases. A similar conclusion was made by Bertels et al. (2015), who noticed the same problem during researching the medical sector. All the enterprises sell to other enterprises, but the end-user is usually a private person, or in the case of Pipedrive Ltd., a single salesperson. This notion needs further research.

References

Afuah, A. (2004). *Business models: A strategic management approach*. New York: McGraw-Hill/Irwin.

A. Le Coq. Home page. Retrieved from: https://www.alecoq.ee/. (Access: 7.11.2019).

Bertels, H.M., Koen, P.A., Elsum, I. (2015). Business models outside the core: Lessons learned from success and failure. *Research-Technology Management, 58(2)*, pp. 20–29. Doi.org/10.5437/08956308X5802294.

Blind, K. (2007). Intellectual property in software development: Trends, strategies and problem. *Review of Economic Research on Copyright Issues, 4(1)*, pp. 15–25. Retrieved from: https://ssrn.com/abstract=997190. (Access: 18.11.2019).

Camino, S., Manenti, F.M. (2015). *Intellectual property and innovation in information and communication technology (ICT)*. JRC Science and Policy Reports. European Commission.

Chesbrough, H. (2003a). *Open innovation: The new imperative for creating and profiting from technology*. Boston: Harvard Business School Press.

Chesbrough, H. (2003b). The logic of open innovation: Managing intellectual property. *California Management Review, 45(3)*, pp. 33–58. Doi. org/10.2307/41166175.

Chesbrough, H. (2006). *Open business models: How to thrive in the new innovation landscape*. Boston: Harvard Business School Press.

Chesbrough, H. (2010). Business model innovation: Opportunities and barriers. *Long Range Planning, 43(2–3)*, pp. 354–363. Doi.org/10.1016/j.lrp.2009.07.010.

Chesbrough, H., Rosenbloom, S.R. (2002). The role of the business model in capturing value from innovation: Evidence from Xerox Corporation's technology spin-off companies. *Industrial and Corporate Change, 11(3)*, pp. 529–555. Doi.org/10.1093/icc/11.3.529.

Cleveron. Homepage. Retrieved from: https://cleveron.com/. (Access: 06.10.2019).

Drucker, P. (1994). The theory of the business. *Harvard Business Review*, September-October, pp. 95–104. Retrieved from: https://hbr.org/1994/09/the-theory-of-the-business. (Access: 10.11.2019).

Estonian Entrepreneurship University of Applied Sciences. Homepage. Retrieved from: https://www.eek.ee/k%C3%B5rgharidus/eriala/robootikatarkvara_arendus. (Access: 11.11.2019).

Global Innovation Index. Homepage. Retrieved from: https://www.globalinnovationindex.org/Home. (Access: 23.09.2019).

Kelli, A., Mets, T., Hoffmann, T. (2013). *Ettevõtlusmudelite ja lepinguvabaduse ulatuse analüüs intellektuaalse omandi kontekstis: majanduslikud ja juriidilised aspektid.* Retrieved from: https://www.just.ee/sites/www.just.ee/files/elfinder/article_files/lepinguvabaduse_analuus_0.pdf. (Access: 15.09.2019).

Knight, G.A., Cavusgil, S.T. (2004). Innovation, organizational capabilities, and the born-global firm. *Journal of International Business Studies, 35(2),* pp. 124–141. Doi.org/10.1057/palgrave.jibs.8400071.

Kuźnar, A., Folfas, P. (2018). How does the protection of intellectual property rights affect Hi-Tech exports from the most advanced economies? *Argumenta Oeconomica, 41(2),* pp. 277–296. Doi.org/10.15611/aoe.2018.2.12.

Linder, J., Cantrell, S. (2001). *Changing business models: Surveying the landscape.* (Doctoral dissertation). Cambridge: Accenture Institute for Strategic Change.

Magretta, J. (2002). *Why business models matter.* Harvard Business Review on Business Model Innovation. USA: HBR Publishing Corporation. Retrieved from: https://hbr.org/2002/05/why-business-models-matter. (Access: 23.10.2019).

Mason, C., Brown, R. (2013). *Entrepreneurial ecosystems and growth oriented entrepreneurship.* Background Paper Prepared for the Workshop Organised by the OECD LEED Programme and the Dutch Ministry of Economic Affairs on Entrepreneurial Ecosystems and Growth Oriented Entrepreneurship. The Hague, Netherlands, November 7th.

Mendonca, S., Pereira, T.S., Godinho, M.M. (2004). Trademarks as an indicator of innovation and industrial change. *Research Policy, 33(9),* pp. 1385–1404. Doi.org/10.1016/j.respol.2004.09.005.

Mets, T., Kelli, A. (2011). Are hi-tech "born-global-s" really born global? *Management of Organizations: Systematic Research, 59,* pp. 81–94.

Mets, T. (2013). The role of intellectual property in globalizing business models of knowledge-intensive SMEs. In: R. Oakey, A. Groen, G. Cook, G.P. Van Der Sijde (eds.), *New technology-based firms in the new millennium, 10.* Bingley: Emerald Group Publishing Limited, pp. 53–70. Doi.org/10.1108/S1876-0228(2013)0000010006.

Morris, M.H., Schindehutte, M., Allen, J. (2005). The entrepreneur's business model: Toward a unified perspective. *Journal of Business Research, 58(6),* pp. 726–735. Doi.org/10.1016/j.jbusres.2003.11.001.

Morris, M.H., Schindehutte, M., Richardson, J., Allen, J. (2006). Is the business model a useful strategic concept? Conceptual, theoretical, and empirical insights. *Journal of Small Business Strategy, 17(1),* pp. 27–50.

Onetti, A., Zucchella, A., Jones, M.V., McDougall-Covin, P.P. (2012). Internationalization, innovation and entrepreneurship: Business models for new technology-based firms. *Journal of Management and Government, 16,* pp. 337–368. Doi.org/10.1007/s10997-010-9154-1.

Osterwalder, A., Pigneur, Y. (2009). *Business model generation. A handbook for visionaries, game changers, and challengers.* Chichester: John Wiley and Sons.

Palo, T., Tähtinen, J. (2013). Networked business model development for emerging technology-based services. *Industrial Marketing Management, 42(5)*, pp. 773–782. Doi.org/10.1016/j.indmarman.2013.05.015.

Pipedrive. Home page. Retrieved from: https://www.pipedrive.com/en-gb. (Access: 07.10.2019).

Rossmann, G.R., Rallis, S.F. (1998). *Learning in the field.* London: Sage Publications Ltd.

Schweizer, L. (2005). Concept and evaluation of business models. *Journal of General Management, 31(2)*, pp. 37–56.

Schumpeter, J. (1934). *The theory of economic development.* Cambridge, MA: Harvard University Press.

Spiegel, B. (2017). The relational organization of entrepreneurial ecosystems. *Entrepreneurship Theory and Practice, 41(1)*, pp. 49–72. Doi.org/10.1111/etap.12167.

Slávik, Š., Bednár, R. (2014). Analysis of business models. *Journal of Competitiveness, 6(4)*, pp. 19–40. Doi.org/10.7441/joc.2014.04.02.

Stake, R. (1995). *The art of case study research.* Thousand Oaks, London, New Delhi: Sage Publications Ltd.

Stam, E. (2015). Entrepreneurial ecosystems and regional policy: A sympathetic critique. *European Planning Studies, 23(9)*, pp. 1759–1769. Doi.org/10.1080/09654313.2015.1061484.

Startup Estonia. (2019). Home page. Retrieved from: https://www.startupestonia.ee/blog/deep-dive-into-the-estonian-startup-sector-in-2019. (Access: 05.09.2019).

Steenhuis, H.J., De Bruijn, E.J. (2006). *High technology revisited: Definition and position.* Proceedings from IEEE International Conference on Management of Innovation and Technology.

Teece, D.J. (2010). Business models, business strategy and innovation. *Long Range Planning, 43(2–3)*, pp. 172–194. Doi.org/10.1016/j.lrp.2009.07.003.

Watson, D. (2006). *Business models.* Petersfield: Harriman House Ltd.

Zott, C., Amit, R. (2008). The fit between product market strategy and business model: Implications for firm performance. *Strategic Management Journal, 29(1)*, pp. 1–26. Doi.org/10.1002/smj.642.

Yin, R. (2003). *Case study research: Design and methods.* Thousand Oaks: Sage Publications Ltd.

5

External Conditions of Profitability of Business Models of High-Growth Enterprises

AGATA MESJASZ-LECH AND ANETA WŁODARCZYK

Contents

5.1 Geographical Conditions of the Functioning of High-Growth Enterprises

Developing enterprises are of fundamental importance for improving the condition of modern economies. That confirms the special role of high-growth enterprises (HGEs) in increasing the level of productivity after recession. Even more so, as the enterprises growing faster than the average contribute significantly to the increase in employment and economic development of individual regions (Grinberger and Nehrebecka, 2015).

Business models are seen as important factors in building competitive advantage and creating value for business entities. The type of the adopted business model is determined by many elements such as the near and far environment of an enterprise. New conditions resulting from a dynamically changing environment are the basic cause of the evolution of business models. The conditions are primarily determined by the place of business. Location in a specific place in space determines access to production factors, final recipients, infrastructure, and fiscal solutions.

The following research problem was formulated:

The location of enterprises has a significant impact on their results, and therefore functioning in a given voivodeship translates into the profitability of high-growth business models adopted by enterprises. Research shows that the geographical location of enterprises affects the possibilities in terms of generating knowledge, for example, due to the availability of highly specialized and qualified employees (Stawiarska, 2019).

5.2 Financial Condition of High-Growth Enterprises in Poland

Research conducted in Poland shows that the frequency of occurrence of Business Gazelles in individual voivodeships does not differ significantly from the indicators describing entrepreneurship in individual regions of Poland. Studies also show that among Polish Business Gazelles, the majority are companies of a mixed nature, often combining production and trade activities. Additionally, the fact that 23% of the surveyed companies declare activity related solely to production means that the enterprises with a production profile clearly dominate in the population of business entities (Kraśnicka and Głód, 2016).

The financial condition of enterprises is connected with the effectiveness of their activity. Economic effectiveness refers to the economic and, in particular, financial results of the functioning of an enterprise and is usually reflected in the relationship between costs and revenues. Effectiveness can be considered in two dimensions: market and economic. In the market dimension, effectiveness is customer-oriented and is seen as the ability to offer products with characteristics ensuring full compliance with customer preferences.

The economic dimension of effectiveness focuses on activities and related costs. Determining the effectiveness in the general sense is based on comparing effects and outlays (Kowalska, 1993). In economic terms, effectiveness expresses the effect-expenditure relationship, and achieving a high level of effectiveness is possible through optimal shaping of the size of material and information streams, as well as the structure of processes. Considering processes in terms of profits and outlays makes it possible to build a system where goals are achieved through making the right decisions. The assessment of effectiveness understood in this way is important from the point of view of business models, because its goal is to contribute to increasing customer satisfaction and reducing costs, and thus to increase the competitiveness of the company. The subject literature often indicates the need and significance of measuring effectiveness (cf. Skrzypek, 2000). It can be discussed in the operational or short-term dimension, and it can be presented in the form of turnover profitability ratios, assets, and capital (Skowronek, 2010). The financial result and revenues from the activity of an enterprise determine the profitability of turnover, and the ratio of revenues to the average state of assets determines the productivity of the resources involved. The impact of the completed activities on the profitability of turnover is connected with the reduction of costs and increasing the efficiency of processes affecting the increase in revenues and strengthening the market position. Increased productivity may occur as a result of increased revenues and rational shaping of resources, that is, inventory, receivables, cash, and infrastructure involved in the functioning of the business. Therefore, effectiveness is considered primarily in terms of financial indicators. The business model, on the other hand, is treated as the architecture of the business activity, which can bring an organization's effectiveness by generating income (Knop and Brzóska, 2016). A special emphasis is put on the profit-making nature of the enterprise and the related need to comply with principles of economy as the basis not only for survival but also for the development of the enterprise in the market. The indicators of a company's performance can include net sales growth rate, operating profit margin, investments in fixed assets, investments in working capital, income tax rate, competitive advantage, and cost of capital (Jabłoński, 2016).

5.3 The Methodology of the Assessment of Profitability of Business Models Adopted by Polish High-Growth Enterprises

In order to solve the presented problem, the method of the multi-dimensional statistical analysis was used. A synthetic indicator of the development of HGEs in a given voivodeship which takes into account financial data proving the profitability of the adopted business model was built. The estimated synthetic development indicators made it possible to rank HGEs located in individual voivodeships according to their financial condition to conclude on the profitability of the business models adopted in them. Also, the stability of the position occupied in the ranking for the analyzed groups of HGEs was assessed, which made it possible to indicate Polish voivodeships which were conducive to the development of enterprises in the analyzed period.

The following variables were analyzed:

1. Stimulants:
   - Activity effectiveness ratio (%) reflecting the relation of total revenues to total costs per one HGE.
   - Profitability rate of gross turnover reflecting the relation of gross financial result to total revenues per one HGE.
   - Gross value of fixed assets determining the value of expenditures incurred for their purchase or production, without the deduction of the value of consumption (redemption) per one HGE (the gross value of fixed assets does not include the value of land and the right of perpetual use of land).
   - Short-term investments covering short-term (current) financial assets, in particular, shares and stocks, other securities, loans granted, other short-term financial assets, cash and other cash assets, and other short-term investments per one HGE.
   - Average monthly gross salary per employee (PLN), which includes cash payments paid to employees or other natural persons, constituting expenses incurred by employers to pay for the performed work, regardless of the sources of their financing and regardless of the basis of the employment relationship or other legal relationships or legal

actions on the basis of which work is performed, per one employee of HGE (divided into 12 months – annual data).
- The share of HGEs in the population of active non-financial enterprises which keep accounting books and employ at least ten people (%).
- Share of HGEs employment in total employment (%) expressed as the ratio of the number of people employed in HGEs to the number of people employed in the examined sample of enterprises.

2. Dominants:
- First-degree financial liquidity ratio expressed as the ratio of short-term investments to short-term liabilities (excluding special funds) per one HGE.

The performance indicator was considered to be a stimulus due to the fact that it reflects the rationality of the operation of the business entity. Rational action is an action that leads to a surplus of revenue over costs. Revenues are perceived as effects obtained as a result of conducted activity, costs, on the other hand, as expenditures necessary to obtain these effects.

The gross turnover profitability index determines the ability of a business entity to generate profit. The high level of the indicator means a good financial condition of the entity and the likelihood of its further development.

The gross value of fixed assets was considered to be a stimulus due to the fact that every economic activity requires the possession of fixed assets necessary to conduct the activity. The size and structure of the assets used in the production process determine the economic efficiency (Wasilewski and Zabadała, 2011). In addition, the value of fixed assets is the result of investment outlays of enterprises which have an impact on regional development (Zygmunt, 2015).

In the study it was assumed that short-term investments can be undertaken by entities that are experienced investors, characterized by high security funds and income. HGEs are characterized by a high average annual revenue growth. Therefore, they are looking for investments generating income in short term.

The average monthly gross salary was treated in the analysis as a measure of the value of intellectual capital. Intellectual capital is the basic resource of an economic entity, which is why it is the main factor of its development and market competitiveness. Therefore, the structure of broadly understood remuneration should support the creation and impact of intellectual capital on the development of an enterprise. Modern remuneration policy should encourage employees to achieve strategic goals of business entities, which even requires treating remuneration as an investment in human capital, and not only as a cost (Sokołowski, 2011).

The share of HGEs in the population of active enterprises is desirable because these enterprises contribute to the development of entrepreneurship. They take advantage of market opportunities to start their activities. Research carried out by Polish Agency for Enterprise Development (PAED) showed that there were two main reasons for the emergence of HGEs:

- Willingness to run one's own business and to achieve personal accomplishment while having an idea for a product and financial possibilities.
- A need for change and self-development, taking advantage of an opportunity.

HGEs are able to survive adverse conditions and even achieve growth in the conditions of economic fluctuations. In many cases, this is due to the specifics of their activities such as offering niche products, diversifying prices, customers, or doing the opposite – focusing on a fixed group of customers (Nieć and Zakrzewski, 2016).

The share of HGEs employment in general employment was treated as a stimulus for new jobs in the market.

The data necessary to estimate the value of diagnostic variables describing the financial condition of HGEs and their importance for the development of individual voivodeships in Poland come from the survey of entrepreneurship indicators conducted by the Central Statistical Office (CSO) (Statistics Poland, 2019). The survey covered active non-financial enterprises keeping accounting books in 2013–2017, which employed at least ten people (in 2017, the size of the surveyed statistical sample was 38,059 enterprises). HGEs whose cumulative growth rate of net revenues from sales of products, goods, and materials was at least 72.8% over the period of three consecutive years (3,940 entities) were separated from this group. This means that HGEs were characterized by at least 20% annual growth of net revenues over a three-year period (CSO, 2019, pp. 29–30). The choice of years and variables for the analysis was dictated by the availability and completeness of data in the database of the CSO. The analyses were carried out for voivodeships constituting the basic administrative units in Poland. Treating voivodeships as objects in the analysis is due to the fact that regional policy is becoming more and more important in increasing the effectiveness of innovation policy (Pachura et al., 2014).

It is assumed that the results of the analysis can constitute the basis for undertaking actions aimed at stimulating or strengthening the investment environment for HGEs in individual voivodeships, which should contribute to the increase of their competitiveness.

In empirical analyses, the development pattern method was used. It is one of the methods of linear ordering and makes it possible to replace the description of objects using a number of features with one synthetic feature (Ostasiewicz, 1998). The development pattern method assumes that there is a model object (the so-called pattern) for which each of the diagnostic features assumes the best values. Then the distances of individual objects (Oi, $i = 1, 2, ..., n$) from the model object (Ow) are determined with the use of a binary function with real values, which should meet the following conditions (Kolenda, 2006):

    a. $d(O_1,O_2) \geq 0$ (the distance between objects is always nonnegative).

    b. $d(O_1,O_2) = d(O_2,O_1)$ (the distance between objects meets the condition of symmetry).

    c. $d(O_1,O_2) \leq d(O_1,O_3) + d(O_3,O_2)$ (the distance between objects meets the condition of triangle inequality).

    d. $d(O_1,O_2) = 0 \Leftrightarrow O_1 = O_2$.

Each binary function which meets the conditions (a–d) is called a metric and is used to determine the similarity between objects. The notation $d(O_1,O_2) \leq d(O_1,O_3)$ means that object O_1 is more similar to object O_2 than to object O_3. Different types of metrics are used to measure similarity between objects, with Euclidean metrics being the most popular.

All diagnostic variables included in the analysis should be classified into one of the three categories of variables: stimulants, destimulants, or neutral variables. Neutral variables measured on the quotient scale should be replaced with stimulants using the following transformation:

$$x_{ij} = \frac{\min\left\{nom_j; x_{ij}^N\right\}}{\max\left\{nom_j; x_{ij}^N\right\}}, \tag{5.1}$$

where x_{ij}^N is the value of a j-th neutral variable for an i-th object, nom_j is the nominal value of a j-the variable.

Then the value of each diagnostic variable measured at least on the interval scale is standardized according to the following formula:

$$z_{ij} = \frac{x_{ij} - \bar{x}_j}{s_j}, \left(i = 1, 2, \ldots, n; \ j = 1, 2, ..m\right) \tag{5.2}$$

where x_{ij} are the values of a j-th diagnostic value X_j describing an i-th object O_i; $\bar{x}_j$ is the arithmetic mean of the diagnostic variable X_j; s_j is the standard deviation of the diagnostic variable X_j; z_{ij} are the standardized values of the variable for an i-th object; m is the number of diagnostic variables; n is the number of objects. The Z_j variable with an average equals to 0, and a standard deviation is already measured on the interval scale, so the transformation of diagnostic variables checked their orders of magnitude to the state of comparability (Walesiak, 2011).

In the development pattern method, the key step is to define the reference object (O_w) and the anti-pattern (O_a) whose geometric representation is respective points $z_w = (z_{wj})_{j \in \{1,2,\ldots,m\}}$ and $z_a = (z_{aj})_{j \in \{1,2,\ldots,m\}}$ which has the following coordinates:

$$z_{wj} = \begin{cases} \max_i z_{ij} & \text{for stimulants} \\ \min_i z_{ij} & \text{for destimulants} \end{cases} \tag{5.3}$$

$$z_{aj} = \begin{cases} \min_i z_{ij} & \text{for stimulants} \\ \max_i z_{ij} & \text{for destimulants} \end{cases} \tag{5.4}$$

The synthetic measure of development (SMD) (m_i) for an i-th object is determined according to the relation of Equations (5.5) and (5.6):

$$m_i = 1 - \frac{d(z_{ij}, z_{wj})}{d(z_{aj}, z_{wj})}, (i = 1, 2, \ldots, n)$$ (5.5)

$$d(z_{ij}, z_{wj}) = \sqrt{\sum_{j=1}^{m} (z_{ij} - z_{wj})^2}, (i = 1, 2, \ldots, n)$$ (5.6)

where $d(z_{ij}, z_{wj})$ is the distance between the i-th object and the model object measured using Euclidean metric; $d(z_{aj}, z_{wj})$ is the distance between the development pattern and the anti-pattern.

The synthetic measure of development has values in the range $(0,1)$, and the closer its values are to unity, the more the i-th object is similar to the model object, and at the same time less similar to the anti-pattern (Ostasiewicz, 1998).

In order to check whether the SMDs estimated in different units of time for the same statistical population are similar to the Friedman rank test was used, the following set of hypotheses was formulated:

$$H_0 : F_1(x) = F_2(x) = \ldots = F_r(x),$$

$$H_1 : \exists \iota, \kappa \in \{1, 2, \ldots, r\} \wedge \iota \neq \kappa : F_\iota(x) \neq F_\kappa(x),$$

where $Fj(x)$ is a distribution function of the SMD for the examined group of objects in the j-th unit of time; r is the number of rankings; and n is the number of examined objects.

The test statistics has the following form (Domański and Pruska, 2000):

$$F = \frac{12}{r(r+1)n} \sum_{j=1}^{r} R_j^2 - 3(r+1)n,$$ (5.7)

where $R_j^2 = \sum_{i=1}^{n} r_{ij}$ is the sum of ranks assigned to objects according to the value of the synthetic measure of development in a j-th time unit $(j = 1, 2, \ldots, r)$. Assuming that the null hypothesis is true, the statistics in the Friedman test have an asymptotic distribution of chi-square with $k-1$ degrees of freedom.

In a situation where the Friedman rank test results indicate the occurrence of significant differences in the total distribution of the values of the SMD for the examined group of objects, it is also worth checking in which time units the greatest differences in the formation of this measure occurred. To this end, the Wilcoxon rank test can be used in which the following hypotheses are made:

$$H_0 : F_i(x) = F_j(x)\ (i \neq j \wedge i, j \in \{1, 2, \dots, r\})$$

$$H_1 : F_i(x) \neq F_j(x)$$

The Wilcoxon test determines the differences between the values of the SMD in two different time units ($SMD_{ik} - SMD_{jk}$), for each tested object ($k = 1, 2, \dots, n$). The modules of these differences are given ranks for which the rank test is defined (Domański and Pruska, 2000):

$$T = \min(T^+, T^-), \tag{5.8}$$

where

$$T^+ = \sum_{x_k > 0} rank\,|x_k| = \sum_{x_k > 0} rank\,|SMD_{ik} - SMD_{jk}|, \tag{5.9}$$

and

$$T^- = \sum_{x_k < 0} rank\,|x_k| = \sum_{x_k < 0} rank\,|SMD_{ik} - SMD_{jk}|, \tag{5.10}$$

where SDM_{ik} is a variable describing the value of the synthetic measure of development in the i-th period for the k-th object.

The set of critical values of the Wilcoxon test is defined by the following relation: $P(T \leq T_\alpha) = \alpha$ (Domański and Pruska, 2000).

For a sample sizes above 25 ($n > 25$), the following test statistics are used (Domański and Pruska, 2000):

$$U_W = \frac{T - E(T)}{D(T)} = \frac{T - \frac{1}{4}n(n+1)}{\sqrt{\frac{1}{24}n(n+1)(2n+1)}}, \tag{5.11}$$

which has an asymptotically normal distribution $N(0,1)$ with the assumption about the truth of the null hypothesis.

The last stage of the analysis is ranking objects according to the decreasing values of the synthetic measure of development in each tested unit of time. Based on the rankings, the values of Spearman and Kendall tau rank correlation coefficients will be determined, for which nonparametric tests will be carried out to verify their statistical significance. On the basis of this conclusion about the stability in the time of ranking, objects in subsequent rankings will be drawn. To verify the null hypothesis about the independence of positioning of objects according to the value of the synthetic measure of development in two selected years:

$$H_0 : \rho_S \left(SMD_\iota, SMD_\kappa \right) = 0, \left(\iota \neq \kappa \wedge \iota, \kappa \in \{1, 2, .., k\} \right)$$

$$H_1 : \rho_S (SMD_\iota, SMD_\kappa) \neq 0,$$

the following statistics needs to be estimated (Piłatowska, 2006):

$$U_S = r_S \cdot \sqrt{n-1}, \tag{5.12}$$

and

$$r_S = 1 - \frac{6 \cdot \Sigma_{i=1}^{n} d_i^2}{n \cdot (n^2 - 1)}, \tag{5.13}$$

where ρ_s is the Spearman rank correlation coefficient for a population; U_S is the test statistics, which for a number of observations higher than 10 ($n \geq 10$) has an asymptotically normal distribution $N(0,1)$; r_s is the Spearman rank correlation coefficient estimator; and d_i is the difference between the positioning of an i-th object in the rankings for the periods ι and κ.

When examining the difference between the probability that the positions of the examined objects in the rankings relative to the synthetic measure of development in two arbitrary units of time are in the same order, and the probability that their order will be different, the Kendall tau correlation coefficient should be estimated (Szajt, 2014):

$$\tau_K = \frac{2(P - Q)}{n \cdot (n - 1)}, \tag{5.14}$$

where τ_K is the Kendall tau coefficient; P is the number of observation pairs for which the relations between positions occupied by any two objects in both rankings are compatible (i.e., if in the first ranking the position occupied by the i-th object is higher than the position occupied by the j-th object, in the second ranking the position of the i-th object will be higher than the position of the j-th object as well); and Q is the number of pairs of not compatible observations for which the relations are opposite.

When verifying the null hypothesis about the irrelevance of the Kendall tau correlation coefficient in the context of the alternative hypothesis indicating the significance of the difference between the probabilities of the appearance of consistent and opposite object arrangements in the rankings:

$$H_0 : \tau_K = 0,$$

$$H_1 : \tau_K \neq 0,$$

the following statistics should be estimated (Szajt, 2014):

$$U_K = \frac{|P - Q| - 1}{\sqrt{\frac{n \cdot (n-1) \cdot (2n+5)}{18}}}, \qquad (5.15)$$

where U_K is the test statistics, which for the number of observations higher than 10 ($n \geq 10$) has an asymptotically normal distribution $N(0,1)$.

5.4 Cost-Effectiveness of the Business Models Adopted by High-Growth Enterprises – A Multidimensional Analysis

On the basis of the set of diagnostic variables constructed for the purpose of this study, the values of the SMD were determined in accordance with formulas (1)–(5), which are presented in Table 5.1.

The analysis of the values of the synthetic measure of development in the years 2013–2017 shows that individual voivodeships in Poland differed in terms of the financial condition of HGEs located in them. The voivodeships with the highest values of the synthetic measure of development in 2013 were Małopolskie (0.6227), Pomorskie (0.5604),

Table 5.1   The Values of the Synthetic Development Measure and Ranking of Voivodeships According to the Value of the Synthetic Measure of Development in the Years 2013–2017

VOIVODESHIP	VOIVODESHIP POSITION IN THE RANKING ACCORDING TO SMD					SYNTHETIC MEASURE OF DEVELOPMENT				
	2013	2014	2015	2016	2017	2013	2014	2015	2016	2017
Dolnośląskie	4	2	5	3	2	0.4441	0.5320	0.4814	0.5500	0.4039
Kujawsko-Pomorskie	12	14	13	14	13	0.2592	0.2462	0.3345	0.2706	0.1877
Lubelskie	15	9	16	16	16	0.1573	0.3345	0.1282	0.2002	0.1657
Lubuskie	10	12	12	10	11	0.2709	0.3268	0.3366	0.3443	0.2080
Łódzkie	8	11	8	7	8	0.3151	0.3319	0.4026	0.4374	0.3062
Małopolskie	1	6	6	5	4	0.6227	0.4125	0.4505	0.5256	0.3742
Mazowieckie	6	5	4	4	1	0.3884	0.4422	0.5269	0.5449	0.4142
Opolskie	9	13	11	15	15	0.2763	0.3064	0.3389	0.2060	0.1681
Podkarpackie	7	16	15	12	10	0.3386	0.1795	0.2661	0.3128	0.2301
Podlaskie	14	7	9	9	9	0.2022	0.3846	0.3898	0.3666	0.2886
Pomorskie	2	1	3	2	3	0.5604	0.5537	0.5315	0.5545	0.3892
Śląskie	3	3	1	1	6	0.4839	0.5266	0.5781	0.5855	0.3339
Świętokrzyskie	16	15	14	13	5	0.1096	0.2419	0.2912	0.2904	0.3386
Warmińsko-Mazurskie	11	10	10	11	14	0.2667	0.3328	0.3513	0.3210	0.1736
Wielkopolskie	13	8	7	8	7	0.2430	0.3826	0.4463	0.4271	0.3194
Zachodniopomorskie	5	4	2	6	12	0.3900	0.4853	0.5461	0.5095	0.1990

and Śląskie (0.4839). The best conditions for the development of HGEs in 2013 were present in the Małopolskie voivodeship, as the enterprises from this voivodeship achieved the optimal level of the financial liquidity ratio (close to the median value of 24%), the highest indicators: performance effectiveness (109.7%), turnover profitability (9%), the gross value of fixed assets (PLN 62.3 million per enterprise), and also had a significant share in creating jobs (17.4% share in total employment in all enterprises from the voivodeship surveyed by CSO). For this reason, the synthetic measure of development for this voivodeship in 2013 is the closest to benchmark value 1 which corresponds to the reference object. In the following three years, Pomorskie and Śląskie voivodeships also occupied the highest positions in rankings describing the financial condition of HGEs. The values of the SMD were in the range of 0.5315–0.5545 for the Pomorskie voivodeship and 0.5266–0.5855 for the Śląskie voivodeship, which turned out to be one of the highest in the studied group of HGEs. Enterprises from the Pomorskie and Śląskie voivodeships in the years 2013–2016 were characterized by relatively high values of the indicators of: performance (106–108%), turnover profitability (5–7%), and gross fixed assets per one enterprise (Śląskie) compared to other enterprises, as well as a high liquidity ratio (the Pomorskie voivodeship). Employment in HGEs also had a significant share in the total employment in all surveyed entities in the Pomorskie and Śląskie voivodeships (15–18% in 2013, 13–14% in 2016). In 2017, the highest values of the synthetic measure of development were found in the following voivodeships: Mazowieckie (0.4142), Dolnośląskie (0.4039), and Pomorskie (0.3892). It is worth noting that the Dolnośląskie voivodeship continually occupied high positions in the SMD rankings which in the consecutive years of the 2013–2017 period were: 4 (SMD = 0.4441), 2 (SMD = 0.5320), 5 (SMD) = 0.4814), 3 (SMD = 0.55), and 2 (SMD = 0.4039). Mazowieckie voivodeship owes the highest ranking position in 2017 to high indicators describing the gross value of fixed assets (PLN 29.5 million/enterprise) and short-term investments (PLN 13.5 million/enterprise), as well as a high average salary (PLN 5,570 per employee per month) and the highest share of HGEs in the studied group of enterprises (11.61%) compared to other voivodeships.

The worst positions in the rankings in 2013 and in the years 2015–2017 were occupied by the Lubelskie voivodeship with the estimated synthetic measure of development in the range of 0.1282–0.2002. The deteriorating financial condition of the HGEs in this voivodeship is indicated by low values of the financial liquidity ratio (15–17%), low short-term investments (PLN 1.89–2.16 million/enterprise), and one of the lowest remuneration level in the group of surveyed enterprises monthly (2,910–3,250 PLN on average/employee). In addition, HGEs in the Lubelskie voivodeship do not have a significant impact on the development of the region as in other Polish voivodeships. They constitute from 6% to 7% of all surveyed enterprises, and people working in these enterprises constitute from 5% to 8.5 % of employee population in this voivodeship. In the years 2016–2017, Opolskie voivodeship also performed unfavorably in the rankings with the value of the synthetic measure of development of 0.2060 and 0.1681, respectively. HGEs located in the Opolskie voivodeship encountered the biggest problems with maintaining financial liquidity (financial liquidity ratio of 10–11%, significantly below the median), as well as turnover profitability (the lowest values of the ratio 1.9–2.2% among all HGEs in Poland). Also, in terms of efficiency, HGEs from the Opolskie voivodeship had the worst results with the index of 102% indicating relatively low total revenues compared to total costs incurred. It is worth noting the group of HGEs from the Podkarpackie and Świętokrzyskie voivodeships. Their rankings gradually began to improve in the last two years. Especially in the light of the fact that the synthetic measure of development for Świętokrzyskie voivodeship in 2013 reached the lowest value of 0.1096, which was the closest value to the anti-pattern. In 2017, HGEs from the Świętokrzyskie voivodeship significantly improved their overall financial condition by increasing business efficiency (from 103.5% in 2013 to 123% in 2017), increasing turnover profitability (from 3.4% to 18.3%), and increasing short-term investments (from PLN 2.3 to 11 million/enterprise).

The charts in the box plots presented in Figure 5.1 show selected descriptive statistics for the estimates of synthetic measures of development in the years 2013–2017. They indicate a growing trend in the SMD value, and, accordingly, a gradual improvement in the financial condition of HGEs in Poland in the years 2013–2016. In 2013, an average voivodeship in Poland was characterized by a development index of 0.333, while in 2016 the average value of this indicator was 0.4029. For half of Polish voivodeships, the synthetic development rate reached at least 0.2957 in 2013 and 0.3969 in 2016. This trend reversed in 2017 when the synthetic measure of development for an average voivodeship in Poland was 0.2813, which is below the average value observed in the years 2013–2016. In half of the voivodeships, the values of the synthetic measure of development in 2017 did not exceed 0.2974. Moreover, the highest level of diversification of Polish voivodeships in terms of the value of the synthetic development indicator was observed in 2013 and the lowest in 2014. Similar trends can be observed for the 25th and 75th percentile values.

In 2013 and 2015 in two voivodeships in Poland, namely, Lubelskie and Świętokrzyskie (2013) and Lubelskie and Podkarpackie (2015), SMDs had values below the lower limit of a typical variation area (0.1915–2013, 0.2800–2015). In 2017, the synthetic development indicators did not reach the lower value of a typical area of variation (0.1909) in as many as four voivodeships: Lubelskie, Opolskie, Warmińsko-Mazurskie, and Kujawsko-Pomorskie, despite the fact that their values were lower than in previous years. In 2013, on the

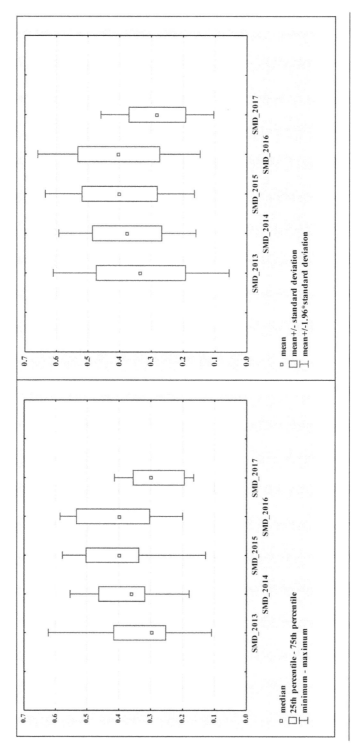

Figure 5.1   The box plots for the estimates of synthetic measures of development in the years 2013–2017.

other hand, the values of the synthetic measure exceeded the upper limit of a typical variability area (0.4745) in the case of Małopolskie, Pomorskie, and Śląskie voivodeships. In 2015, the upper limit of a typical variation in the value of the synthetic measure of development increased to the level of 0.5200, and yet it was exceeded by four voivodeships: Śląskie, Zachodniopomorskie, Pomorskie, and Mazowieckie. In 2017, SMD values higher than the upper limit of a typical variability area (0.3716) were recorded in four voivodeships: Mazowieckie, Dolnośląskie, Pomorskie, and Małopolskie.

To sum up the above considerations, it should be emphasized that in all voivodeships and in all of the analyzed years, the estimated values of the SMD were significantly different from unity. In 2017, the values were even closer to the anti-pattern value than to the reference object. This means that none of Polish voivodeships can be treated as a reference object due to the conditions of the development of HGEs. In the majority of voivodeships in Poland, the overall financial condition of HGEs deteriorated in 2017 compared to previous years, which may be a warning signal for decision makers developing the region's economic development strategy.

In the next step of the analysis, the assumption that in particular voivodeships in Poland there were similar conditions conducive to the development of HGEs over several years was checked using the Friedman rank test. This test is a nonparametric equivalent of a univariate analysis of variance with repeatable measurement, which is why it was selected to examine the differences between five dependent variables (SMD2013, SMD2014, SMD2015, SMD2016, and SMD2017) corresponding to synthetic measures of development in the years 2013–2017 (cf. King and Minium, 2009).

The results of Friedman rank test for SMD values (25,450) which are presented in Table 5.2 indicate the occurrence of significant differences in the distribution of the values of the synthetic measure in the years 2013–2017 at the significance level of 0.01. This means that the conditions for the development of HGEs in Polish voivodeships changed in the analyzed years, which is indicated by significantly different values of the measure describing the financial condition of these enterprises in five consecutive years. It can be concluded, therefore, that the location of HGEs significantly affects the financial results they achieve, and, accordingly, the functioning of an enterprise in

Table 5.2 Wilcoxon and Friedman Rank Test for the Synthetic Development Measure and Rankings of Voivodeships According to the Value of the Synthetic Measure of Development in the Years 2013–2017

SMD (BASE YEAR)_SMD	WILCOXON TEST FOR SMD			WILCOXON TEST FOR RANKINGS		
(ANALYZED YEAR)	T	Z	P-VALUE	T	Z	P-VALUE
SMD2013_SMD2014	32.000	1.862	0.063	59.500	0.028	0.977
SMD2013_SMD2015	**22.000**	**2.379**	**0.017**	55.500	0.256	0.798
SMD2013_SMD2016	**18.000**	**2.585**	**0.011**	44.000	0.105	0.917
SMD2013_SMD2017	34.000	1.758	0.079	53.500	0.369	0.712
SMD2014_SMD2015	**28.000**	**2.068**	**0.039**	40.500	0.349	0.727
SMD2014_SMD2016	33.000	1.810	0.070	48.500	0.251	0.802
SMD2014_SMD2017	**12.000**	**2.896**	**0.004**	57.500	0.142	0.887
SMD2015_SMD2016	59.000	0.465	0.642	35.000	0.314	0.754
SMD2015_SMD2017	**5.000**	**3.258**	**0.001**	26.500	0.102	0.919
SMD2016_SMD2017	**3.000**	**3.361**	**0.001**	44.500	0.070	0.944
Friedman rank ANOVA test						
Friedman test statistics – SMD	**25.450**		**p-value**		**0.00004**	
Friedman test statistics – rankings of voivodeships	0.12329		**p-value**		0.99818	

Note: N is the number of unrelated and important cases (N = 16); T is the critical value of Wilcoxon test for group size n ≤ 25; Z is the critical value of Wilcoxon test for group size n > 25; p-value is the significance level of the test result. The results in bold are statistically significant at the 0.05 significance level.

a given province translates into the profitability of business models adopted by enterprises. To check in which year the values of the SMD differed the most from the other estimates, the Wilcoxon signed rank test for matched pairs was performed for each pair of dependent variables (cf. Table 5.2). Significant differences in the distribution of the synthetic measures at the significance level of 0.01 were identified for the years 2014 and 2017, 2015 and 2017, and 2016 and 2017. At the significance level of 0.1, on the other hand, the values of the synthetic measure of development in individual voivodeships in Poland did not show significant differences in 2015 and 2016. Therefore, the results of the Wilcoxon test confirmed the previously formulated observations about the occurrence of a general upward trend in the value of the SMD in the years 2013–2016 and a significant decrease in the value of this measure in 2017.

It was also checked, using Friedman rank test and Wilcoxon pair order test, whether rankings of voivodeships carried out for the years 2013–2017 according to the value of the SMD (cf. Table 5.1) would also show differences. At the level of significance of 0.05, it was not confirmed that the positioning of voivodeships in terms of the financial condition of HGEs changed significantly in the years 2013–2017 (cf. Table 5.2). This proves that the position of a given province in the SMD rankings is relatively stable in the analyzed years. Therefore, the changes observed in the financial condition of HGEs located in individual voivodeships in the years 2013–2017 do not affect their position in the rankings (Mesjasz-Lech, 2019).

Spearman rank correlation (5.13) and Kendall tau (5.14) coefficients were also estimated to identify the voivodeships in which the conditions for the development of HGEs were the best in a long-term perspective (cf. Table 5.3).

On the basis of the analysis of the results presented in Table 5.3, one can draw a conclusion about the occurrence of positive and statistically significant correlation relationships between the rankings of voivodeship in the years 2013 and 2017. Only the Kendall tau test

Table 5.3   Spearman Rank Correlation and Kendall Tau Coefficients for Rankings of Voivodeships According to the Value of the Synthetic Measure of Development

VARIABLE	SPEARMAN RANK CORRELATION COEFFICIENT				
	SMD2013	SMD2014	SMD2015	SMD2016	SMD2017
SMD2013	1.0000	**0.6206**	0.7294	**0.7765**	**0.5059**
SMD2014	**0.6206**	1.0000	**0.8647**	**0.8382**	**0.5324**
SMD2015	0.7294	**0.8647**	1.0000	**0.9176**	**0.5794**
SMD2016	**0.7765**	**0.8382**	**0.9176**	1.0000	**0.7735**
SMD2017	**0.5059**	**0.5324**	**0.5794**	**0.7735**	1.0000
	KENDALL TAU COEFFICIENTS				
	SMD2013	SMD2014	SMD2015	SMD2016	SMD2017
SMD2013	1.0000	**0.4167**	**0.5167**	**0.5833**	0.3167
SMD2014	**0.4167**	1.0000	**0.7333**	**0.6333**	**0.3667**
SMD2015	**0.5167**	**0.7333**	1.0000	0.7667	**0.4667**
SMD2016	**0.5833**	**0.6333**	0.7667	1.0000	**0.6000**
SMD2017	0.3167	**0.3667**	**0.4667**	**0.6000**	1.0000

Note: The correlation coefficients in bold are significant for $p < 0.05$.

at the significance level of 0.05 shows no reason to reject the null hypothesis about the lack of correlation relationship between the positioning of voivodeships according to SMD in the extreme years of the analyzed period, that is, in 2013 and 2017. This indicates a similarity in the positioning of voivodeships in the rankings according to the financial condition of the analyzed groups of HGEs. The voivodeships that created favorable conditions for the development of high-growth enterprises in the long term (2013–2017) were Dolnośląskie, Mazowieckie, Pomorskie, and Śląskie; and in the last analyzed year, the conditions for the development of high-growth enterprises deteriorated in the Śląskie voivodeship and improved in the Mazowieckie voivodeship.

5.5 Discussion and Conclusion

HGEs must be flexible to adapt to changing market conditions. A great emphasis must be put on maintaining production continuity and implementing innovative technological and organizational solutions (Krošláková et al., 2015). The business models adopted by the enterprises include the assumption of the necessity of monitoring the external environment and reacting quickly to both alarming signals about the economic downturn or possibilities of political crisis and publicly available information on new regulations being prepared and the availability of external sources of investment financing. This assumption is reflected in making the development strategy more flexible and using the organizational agility of the company to identify opportunities and threats faster than the competition, which allows them to survive in conditions of strong market competition, and also helps build a competitive advantage (Otola, 2013).

It should also be pointed out that the group of Polish HGEs is dominated by small- and medium-sized entities (SMEs) (Statistics Poland, 2019), which are more dependent on their business environment and political environment than large companies. Due to the size of their business operations, SMEs still face barriers which limit their access to strategic production resources or external financing sources, which translated into a change in the structure of HGEs in many countries around the world. After the end of the global financial crisis subprime (2009), the share of HGEs in the group of enterprises from the service sector increased significantly with a simultaneous decrease in their share in the group of production enterprises (Krošláková et al., 2015). The specialization of HGEs in the sectors of services related to professional, scientific, or technical activities, where the size of the enterprise is not so significant in relation to its intellectual capital (skills and knowledge of the employees), are conducive to the processes of digitization and globalization. The development of new digital technologies related to the analysis of large datasets (Big Data), the implementation of artificial intelligence, the progressive process of digitization of the society, and the dissemination of e-office services contribute to the creation of new, digitally enhanced business models. These models are seen as important in building competitive advantage and creating value of business entities by shortening their distance to the market and saving time (OECD SME and Entrepreneurship Outlook, 2019). The conditions for the development of HGEs presented above are strongly determined by the place of activity of an enterprise. The location of an HGE in a given voivodeship in Poland can be important for the profitability of the business model adopted by it. On the other hand, HGEs contribute to the development of the region by creating new jobs and generating positive effects related to the increase of economic activity in the region. Research is also conducted on the role of high-growth innovative companies in ensuring productivity growth and achieving sustainable competitiveness of regions (Vértesy et al., 2017). For this reason, it can be concluded that there is a feedback between the development of voivodeships in Poland and the financial condition of HGEs conducting business activity in a given voivodeship.

The statistical sample of the study aimed at identifying the relationship between the geographical location of enterprises and the profitability of adopted business models was comprised of enterprises located in individual Polish voivodeships. The data referring to the type of a business model, which is connected with the structure of costs and revenue generating mechanisms, was analyzed. The analysis covered only the group of HGEs, as it was assumed that the fast increase in revenue is typical for enterprises that contribute the most to the economic development.

The results of the Friedman rank test indicate the occurrence of significant differences in the distribution of the value of the synthetic measure in the years 2013–2017 describing the financial condition of enterprises in five consecutive years. This means that the location of HGEs significantly affects their financial results, which means that their functioning in a given voivodeship translates into the profitability of business models adopted by enterprises. In addition, a similarity in the positioning of voivodeships in rankings according to financial condition was observed.

References

Domański, Cz., Pruska, K. (2000). *Nieklasyczne metody statystyczne.* Warszawa: PWE.

Grinberger, P., Nehrebecka, N. (2015). Determinanty wzrostu polskich przedsiębiorstw giełdowych. *Ekonomia. Rynek, Gospodarka, Społeczeństwo, 43*, pp. 41–65.

Jabłoński, A. (2016). Longitudinalne badania modeli biznesu przedsiębiorstw. *Zeszyty Naukowe Uniwersytetu Ekonomicznego w Krakowie, 6(954)*, pp. 95–110.

King, B.M., Minium, E.W. (2009). *Statystyka dla psychologów i pedagogów.* Warszawa: Wydawnictwo Naukowe PWN.

Knop, L., Brzóska, J. (2016). Rola innowacji w tworzeniu wartości przez modele biznesu. *Zeszyty Naukowe Politechniki Śląskiej. Seria: Organizacja i Zarządzanie, 99*, pp. 213–232.

Kolenda, M. (2006). *Taksonomia numeryczna. Klasyfikacja, porządkowanie i analiza obiektów wielocechowych.* Wrocław: Wydawnictwo Akademii Ekonomicznej im. Oskara Langego we Wrocławiu.

Kowalska, K. (1993). *Mierniki gospodarowania surowcami i materiałami.* Warszawa: Państwowe Wydawnictwo Ekonomiczne.

Kraśnicka, T., Głód, W. (2016). Determinants of high-growth enterprises in Poland. *Problemy Zarządzania, 14(3/62)*, pp. 49–67.

Krošláková, M., Kubičková, V., Jurkovičová, L., Kubiniy, N. (2015). Dynamics of high-growth enterprises – "gazelles" – in Czech Republic. *Problems and Perspective in Management, 13(2)*, pp. 27–35.

Mesjasz-Lech, A. (2019). Logistics performance of European Union markets: Towards the development of entrepreneurship in the transport and storage sector. *Global Journal of Environmental Science and Management, 5*, pp. 122–130.

Nieć, M., Zakrzewski, R. (2016). *Firmy szybkiego wzrostu. Raport z badań jakościowych.* Retrieved from: https://www.parp.gov.pl/storage/publications/pdf/2016_firmy_szybkiego_wzrostu.pdf. (Access: 25.10.2019)

OECD SME and Entrepreneurship Outlook. (2019). Paris. Retrieved from: https://www.oecdilibrary.org/sites/34907e9cen/1/2/1/index.html?itemId=/content/publication/34907e9cen&mimeType=text/html&_csp_=97b1ca7ff34abaf04c3b6ec7089258c9&itemIGO=oecd&itemContentType=book. (Access: 27.10.2019).

Ostasiewicz, W. (ed.). (1998). *Statystyczne metody analizy danych.* Wrocław: Wydawnictwo Akademii Ekonomicznej im. Oskara Langego we Wrocławiu.

Otola, I. (2013). *Procesy zarządzania przedsiębiorstwami a konkurencyjność w warunkach zarażonego rynku.* Częstochowa: Wydawnictwo Politechniki Częstochowskiej.

Pachura, P., Skowron-Grabowska, B., Ociepa-Kubicka, A. (2014). The evolution and configuration of regional innovation strategies (RIS) – case studies of the visegrad countries (V4). *Acta Universitatis Lodziensis, Folia Oeconomica, 6(308)*, pp. 149–158.

Piłatowska, M. (2006). *Repetytorium ze statystyki.* Warszawa: Wydawnictwo Naukowe PWN.

Skowronek, C. (2010). Procesy logistyczne w kształtowaniu ekonomiki przedsiębiorstw. In: I. Bonk (ed.), *Logistyka w naukach o zarządzaniu. Księga poświęcona pamięci profesora Mariana Sołtysika.* Katowice: Wydawnictwo Uniwersytetu Ekonomicznego w Katowicach.

Skrzypek, E. (2000). *Jakość i efektywność.* Lublin: Wydawnictwo Uniwersytetu Marii Curie-Skłodowskiej.

Sokołowski, J. (2011). Strategia wynagrodzeń a budowa kapitału intelektualnego przedsiębiorstwa. *Zeszyty Naukowe, Uniwersytet Ekonomiczny w Poznaniu, 172*, pp. 232–241.

Statistics Poland, Selected entrepreneurship indicators in 2013-2017. (2019). Retrieved from: https://stat.gov.pl/obszary-tematyczne/podmioty-gospodarcze-wynikifinansowe/przedsiebiorstwa-niefinansowe/wybrane-wskazniki-przedsiebiorczosci-w-latach-2013-2017,23,6.html. (Access: 24.20.2019).

Stawiarska, E. (2019). *Modele zarządzania innowacjami w łańcuchach i sieciach dostaw międzynarodowych koncernów motoryzacyjnych.* Warszawa: CeDeWu.

Szajt, M. (2014). *Przestrzeń w badaniach ekonomicznych.* Częstochowa: Sekcja Wydawnictw Wydziału Zarządzania Politechniki Częstochowskiej.

Vértesy, D., Del Sorbo, M., Damioli, G. (2017). *High-growth, innovative enterprises in Europe.* Luxembourg: EUR 28606 EN, Publications Office for the European Union.

Walesiak, M. (2011). *Uogólniona miara odległości GDM w statystycznej analizie wielowymiarowej z wykorzystaniem programu R.* Wrocław: Wydawnictwo Uniwersytetu Ekonomicznego.

Wasilewski, M., Zabadała, P. (2011). Wartość i zużycie środków trwałych w ujęciu sektorowym. *Zeszyty Naukowe Szkoły Głównej Gospodarstwa Wiejskiego w Warszawie Ekonomika i Organizacja Gospodarki Żywnościowej, 89*, pp. 49–59.

Zygmunt, A. (2015). Nakłady inwestycyjne i wartość brutto środków trwałych przedsiębiorstw - analiza porównawcza w ujęciu powiatów województwa opolskiego. *Zeszyty Naukowe Wyższej Szkoły Bankowej we Wrocławiu, 15(7)*, pp. 953–960.

6

Analyzing the Employer Branding Business Models Based on Primary Research Results

Ágnes Csiszárik-Kocsir and Mónika Garai-Fodor

Contents

6.1 Introduction

Differences between the various generations were always present at workplaces. This phenomenon exists for a long time since different generations perceive the same workplace or task differently, and also evaluate the conditions offered by employers differently. However, it is a fact that the gap has never been so great between the active generations working at the same workplace, as it is today. One reason behind this change is that the industrial society has been gradually replaced by an information- and then by a knowledge-based society, which has completely rearranged the system of communication between people. Internet makes the obtaining of information easier; however, it changes the nature of the relation between people, and results in generational conflicts never seen before. The information society created a virtual society as well. Younger generations are brought up within this virtual society, and this is the place where they are able to act confidently. More confidently than in the real world. Older generations therefore often feel excluded from this new world.

Employers find it difficult to offer tasks and an atmosphere which would be optimal, attractive, and inspirational for employees with different value systems and different socialization backgrounds. It is not by chance that in the past years, a number of researches have been conducted on how the ranking of employee motivational tools had changed, considering the fact that the HR profession experiences this change to an increasingly greater extent.

Generation researchers define generations based on the cohort experiences of youth age: the mutual experiences, which could later influence the shaping of the personality and value system of the age group (Törőcsik, 2003). Researches claim that the economic-social environment in which that particular generation was socialized is a rather important aspect. The impulses, influences they have experienced, or the objects characterizing their environment, and the events defining their lives greatly contribute to their performance on the labor market, and attitude toward work and career. Accordingly, professional literature reveals the following generational peculiarities (Tari, 2011):

6.1.1 Veteran Generation

They usually work for one employer, in one field, throughout their life. It is true that they have built a new world, in which they have gathered valuable knowledge and experience; however, many times they stick to solutions which worked for them in the past. Their presence on the labor market is not typical today.

6.1.2 Baby-Boomer Generation

They desire new ways, knowledge, information, and action; they build careers. This is what makes them different from their parents. They are the great rebels, the "flower children" of the '70s, who wanted to live in peace and happiness. Then, they grew up and started to work. Though they still question the world created by their parents, sometimes the old habits they were taught emerge. Today, they are characterized by discipline, respect, and persistence. They are attached to their workplace and their desks. Horizontal career paths have great importance for them.

6.1.3 Generation X

They are the messenger, or transient generation. They have encountered the world of Internet already in their teens and youth age, and their work and life is basically defined by the web. Most of them are typical "salary men," who let others tell them what to do and how; they follow the company rules to the letter and become incorporated into the organization. Nevertheless, they are able to renew themselves again and again and keep up with the fast pace of today's world. The name X does not only refer to the people, but also to a certain kind of social hierarchy, in which people are prisoners of the sacred triad of status, money, and social ladder, with an emotionally and intellectually empty life. Members of generation X are not those ripped jeans kids who "sleep together out of wedlock, did not learn that in God we trust, and do not respect the Queen and their parents," as quoted by the Time magazine in 1990. Generation X is at the peak of its performance now. Their knowledge, experience, wisdom, discipline in work, and loyalty represent such a value which could make a company of any type and size one of the top ones.

6.1.4 Generation Y

They are the first wave of the digital generations; Internet is present in their everyday lives. Generation Y brings a serious challenge for the labor market since they represent a new level of quality compared to their predecessors, the messenger generation. They confront long-existing rules with an even greater confidence than that of the previous generation, and they also have different abilities. Esoteric literature says that they are on a mission; their task is to open the spiritual eye of mankind and to form a critical mass with the duty to initiate changes.

They grew up together with computers; they are quite practical and know their way well around the Internet. Generation Y shapes and forms the workplace themselves to fit their needs. The millennium generation wants to enjoy their workplace; it should be modern, different from ordinary, with spacious rooms, and with a kitchen to spend meals together while chatting (Ali and Szikora, 2017).

6.1.5 Generation Z

Members of generation Z – the target group of our primary research project – were entirely born into the world which is more and more defined by the various digital technologies, they are the IT or Digital X (DY) generation. Generation Z, who entered the labor market in the first years of the 21st century, is characterized by rapid changes. It is not by chance that they got their name from the expression "zappers," or "switcher, hopper." They live their lives in a much faster pace than their predecessors, and if there is something they do not like – such as a job – they are ready to change it immediately. Compared to the previous generations, they represent an entirely different world: modern technology, IT, and the online world reached the adult age at the same time with them, becoming a part of their personalities. They live their social relations in the real and virtual world at the same time. For them, it comes natural that their everyday communication, emotional and social life, creative spirit, and playfulness are performed on the Internet, with the help of mobile phones and other digital devices, with each other, and shared in front of the greatest audience (Facebook, Twitter, iwiw…). Members of the digital X generation practically never knew a world without Internet, telecommunication, or television. Maybe this is why they are battling with the lack of interpersonal skills, and the inability for active listening?

6.2 Characteristics of Generation "Z" as Workforce

Job-hopping is natural for generation Z. They move on without compromises; they are jumping between workplaces just like a monkey jumps from tree to tree, anytime they feel like they need to; they will not get stuck at a company; they will not worry about having a steady income or a fix desk somewhere. They are brave, initiative, and they have less doubt regarding their own abilities and limitations. They have a practical mindset, and they appreciate the freedom of the individual, and indirect, informal environments. They are building a new world, since they do not represent a traditional office work culture, as they are able to perform their tasks in any part of the world with the help of Internet, and they create their own virtual communities. Spiritual literature identifies them as the star or crystal generation. They are characterized by being rather smart than wise, and they feel comfortable in the world of technology. They are not good with words and emotions, and they are able to realize their desires even if the cost is high. They will not implement their revolutionary ideas individually, but they will rather serve the society in collaboration with each other. About 97% of young people considers the protection of the environment to be important, and 74% of them already practices green behaviors such as recycling or selective waste collection and purchasing energy-saving light bulbs. When having to choose between two workplaces, they rather prefer the one with a conscious corporate social responsibility (CSR) strategy and an environment-conscious way of thinking (Ridderstrale, 2004).

For members of the digital generation, personal relations are decisive, and they use the Internet as a tool facilitating the maintenance of existing friendships and relations. The five most attractive occupations according to them are veterinarians, teachers, policemen, doctors, and of course football players, though 64% of them aspires to become their own boss as an adult instead of having to work for somebody. This is an important information for companies. They will have to establish such an organizational structure and culture which supports individual work and has a flat hierarchy. The trend of "flattening" of organizations will continue in the beginning of the 21st century. Compared to the size of the organization, the levels within the hierarchy will decrease. The number of employees reporting to a single leader, and the number of employees supervised by the leader will increase; however, hierarchical levels will disappear. The number of positions reporting to the CEO will grow, while the number of hierarchical levels in between will fall. Divisional leaders will get closer and closer to the CEO; they will work under a tougher control, but at the same time for a higher salary, and with an incentive that stimulates their long-term interest (Kissné, 2010; Tari, 2010).

6.3 Method

In the framework of the project, we analyzed the factors influencing the career and job choice of the Z generation through qualitative and quantitative techniques in the context of consumer and expert surveys. We also reviewed the opinions of the HR specialists on the employer's side in the framework of expert interviews. Our goal is to provide points to help employers focusing on Z generation to effectively pursuit a target group-oriented employer branding strategy, as well as to examine employer expectations and selection methods and compare the differences between them.

The first phase of the research project was the qualitative examinations. In the frame of that, we made focus-group interviews with the members of Z generation to establish the standardized questionnaire used during the second quantitative research step and qualitative expert interviews with HR and employer branding experts, to identify the employer's ideas about the characteristics of the Z generation. In the frame of qualitative phase, we made focus-group interviews with the member of Z generation, as a potential employee. We conducted 30 mini-focus interviews, using semi-structured interview guides and snowball sampling method, the only recruiting condition was that all interviewees should be the member of Z generation. A recording of the interviews was made. The results were processed using a traditional content analysis methodology.

The main research questions of that qualitative phase were as follows:

- What does the generation think about career, success, and the preferred and disadvantaged workplace?

- What does their career and success in work mean? What factors help them achieve their individual goals most effectively?
- How can the career goals that they formulate be achieved?
- What do they expect from a good job? Which employer's activities and programs may be the most target group-specific for them?
- What kind of generation problems do the members of the sample perceive? How open are they to work with other generations? What are its advantages and disadvantages?

The other parallel qualitative research step was the expert interview with the HR and employer branding experts. The recruiting of the subjects was also done with the snowball method in this case: interviewing automotive suppliers, manufacturing and development companies – HR managers of large and multinational companies and conducting interviews with HR specialists. All five companies were located in Hungary but were foreign-owned: two operate in the capital city, one in Békés, one in Csongrád, and one in Veszprém County. Of the companies participating in the research, the smallest number of people employed was 300, the largest being 3,700 full-time employees.

Our goal was to get to know the challenges and difficulties faced by practitioners in the labor market and what they experience regarding generational differences.

- What are the methods applied to address the Z generation?
- Are there any HR or HR communication techniques, activities, campaigns that were judged effective on the basis of their empirical experience, and would they recommend them to other employers wishing to open up to the Z generation?

In the second phase, the quantitative survey was implemented. Again, the non-representative snowball method was applied during the sampling process, and we recruited respondents with the same filter criteria regarding their age. Throughout the conduction of the survey, we have used a standardized questionnaire designed by the results of the qualitative survey. With the application of the computer-assisted personal interviewing (CAPI) method, we have received 1,178 valid questionnaires as a result of the survey. The partial results of the first phase of the research project are introduced in the previous studies. In this present study, we demonstrate how the partial results of the project compare the employer and employees' ideas related to the research questions.

6.4 Findings

6.4.1 What Does the Z Think about the Conditions of Entering the World of Work?

In the frame of qualitative research, we were interested in what young people think about the conditions of entering the world of work, and how do they perceive their own opportunities in the labor market. Young people agreed in the fact that it is difficult to find a job, and it is even harder to find a proper workplace.

The majority of respondents claimed that a higher level of education means a greater challenge in finding a suitable workplace.

They also thought that it is easier for those with a valuable social capital, or those who studied a profession where there is a shortage of skilled experts. On the other hand, people with a lower level of qualification and motivation have a harder time finding a job, according to youngsters.

"It is easier for those who have a higher level of educational attainment, and a wider circle of relations, and also if the number of people working within their field of occupation is relatively low. It is more difficult for those with a lower level of education, who lack motivation, and who are also looking for a job in a field which is already full." As future employees, the greatest challenge according to respondents is to find a job which makes them happy, and which is also a lucrative one. They believe that finding and maintaining the proper balance between work and free time will later become a problem.

More people said that seeing the example of their parents, the balance in many cases shifted in favor of work, and many of them sacrificed their free time or even their health for work. Young people, however, one after another confirmed that they do not intend to follow this example. In a separate topic, we have examined the aspects which generation Z considers in the process of choosing their place of work. The decisive aspects claimed to be of primary importance included working hours as well, besides the salary and allowances. They prefer flexible working hours, it is important for them to have time for themselves. Another important aspect is the atmosphere of the workplace, whether it is an attractive environment, a place where they feel good while performing their work.

Another spontaneously mentioned aspect was the opportunity to move forward, which is considered in quite a conscious manner in the selection process. It is also a matter of importance whether the place enables the implementation of creative ideas and ambitions. Respondents explained that in order to achieve their goals and dreams, they are able and willing to work hard, but only if their efforts are recognized and compensated. Self-fulfilment, self-management, and an inspiring working atmosphere are also significant factors. A number of experts have already highlighted that these young people show the greatest level of sensitivity toward receiving not only a salary, but an identity from the company as well.

6.4.2 What Does It Take to Have a Successful Career? "Is It Surely Only up to Us?"

We have asked students about what they believe to be necessary for a successful career of a young beginner. Many of them emphasized knowledge, determination, and strong motivation.

They feel that in order to be successful in a particular field, one must be persistent, motivated, and determined. However, a number of external factors are also necessary, such as relations: "to be at the right place at the right time," to be able to exploit opportunities, and also that the workplace should enable appropriate opportunities and a suitable environment for career and development. According to participants, a beginner can only be successful today, if he is flexible, able to cope with load, up-to-date, well-informed, enthusiastic and motivated, and can take up the "constant speed" of work and adapt to the expectations demanded by an ever-accelerating world. In obtaining these characteristics and competences, and generally in having a successful start, mentors play a significant role.

Young people agreed that it would be quite useful to have a supporting person (mentor), who would prepare them to be ready for work. They feel that the best possible way to implement this is within the frame of education (as an optional course), or to offer it at an affordable price as a training session, where managing directors, HR experts, and successful people in particular fields would present the most important advices based on their personal experiences. Beginners could receive personalized information and instructions about how they should prepare for an interview as a beginner, and from where they should gather information about job opportunities. What should they take into consideration when having to fit in at a workplace, and what kind of rights and obligations does an employee have, thus receiving practical and useful information and guidance. With the management of such training sessions, corporations might obtain a high level of awareness and recognition from the young generation, who are otherwise quite difficult to reach and persuade. We believe that sponsoring these professional programs could not only serve as an effective means for building relations for an employer who in many cases face the challenge of skills shortage, but it is also an excellent tool to build commitment toward the brand. The currently available alternatives, limited to workshop-like open days and a few hours long ad hoc presentations, do not offer comprehensive solutions. Though these are refreshing initiatives, a systematically built professional program focusing on the requirements of the target group might operate with a much better efficiency. And based on the findings, it seems that the demand from the future employees exists toward such events.

In the following part of the research project, we conducted semi-structured interviews with the members of the employer side. Our goal was to understand what challenges and hardships experts in practice perceive on the labor market, and what they experienced concerning generation gaps. What methods do they employ in order to connect with the Z generation? Do they have any HR, or HR communication techniques, activities, campaigns which they believe to be more effective, based on their empirical experiences? Would they recommend them to other employers wishing to connect with the Z generation?

During the research, we interviewed HR experts from large and international enterprises and HR specialists dealing in recruitment. Recruiting the participants was done with the snowball logic. Each of the five enterprises has Hungarian branches, but all are foreign companies. As for locations, two are in the capital Budapest, and the remaining three are situated in Békés, Csongrád, and Veszprém

Counties, respectively. Among the companies taking part in the research, the smallest one employed 300 personnel, whereas the largest one had 3,700 employees. An important conclusion is that the experts believe that the successful solution for market challenges is cooperation. As part of this, they named the necessity of synchronizing education institutions, expert organizations, and the interests of the companies on the employer side.

As another important pillar, they stressed the importance of taking part in education; in a technological environment which develops quickly, and becomes more specialized each day, companies also have to take part in education. Due to the sector's trends, actual job descriptions will transform in the future, and they also have to prepare their colleagues for this. An excellent opportunity for this is internal courses, advanced courses, and the option of specialization. Generation gap is also a challenging factor, both in recruiting and in keeping qualified, talented personnel. On the side of the employer, this demands an adaptation initiative and flexibility when facing a generation's needs. This makes it necessary to realize that HR and HR communication tools have to be tailored to the employee ranks in question.

While in the case of the Z generation, individual goals, individualism in general, and the possibility of realizing personal career and path of life clearly gained an increase in importance, older generations believe that trustworthiness, stability, and transparency are more important. This is why we need the long-known differentiation of marketing to be adapted to HR as well: identification of the needs of target groups, in this case, employees, and solutions tailored specifically to these needs. Therefore, highly standardized solutions will lose their efficiency in calling out to the employees having more and more heterogeneous demands, and will have less of an effect on keeping them.

6.4.3 How Can an Employer Effectively Motivate Its Z Workers?

In the frame of quantitative research, we analyzed the main motivation of Z generation in case of working. The word motivation – or incentive, inspiration – originates from the Latin word "movere," which means to move, movement (Klein and Klein, 2008).

Motivation provides an explanation for the observable behavior of people. The understanding of the various motivational theories and tools is necessary for the selection of the best incentives and drivers ensuring the most efficient solution in case of employees as well. From the aspect of employer branding and management theory, it is important to know that performance is nothing but the product of abilities multiplied by motivation (Tóthné, 2004). The result of a well-designed incentive plan is the performance expected by the organization and the satisfaction of employees. Leaders are able to have an influence on this, and with the proper range of motivational tools, they are able to generate an efficient stimulation in order to achieve the desired results (Göndör, 2003). Motivation theories were first studied to a deeper extent after the 17th century, and the most popular theories regarding consumer behavior and consumption psychology were drafted in the 20th century (Kópházi, 2007; Tóth, 2009).

After the elaboration of content theories – Maslow, Herzberg – process theories were developed, Vroom, for example, revealed that it is important that workers should feel that they are able to solve the assigned task, and receive a reward for the performed work, which will appeal to them, and provide a motivation throughout the performance of tasks. Furthermore, he also emphasized that during a work process the factors driving a particular person must be taken into account, and the incentive system must be elaborated accordingly. It is important that performance should have to be measurable since that is the only way of providing accurate reward (Garda, 2009; Gonda, 2013).

The efficiency of external rewarding is questioned now by the motivation 3.0 theory. Pink proved that not only biologic and external rewarding can serve as motivation. He highlighted the fact that motivation can also be counterproductive in terms of efficiency; he compared reward to caffeine that keeps people at a fast pace only for a few hours, but after the effect is gone, things will get worse (Pink, 2010). Pink emphasized the importance of internal motives and their motivational impact on the efficiency and productivity of work. Though it is not well known in Hungary, a number of companies in the United States of America apply the results-only working environment (ROWE) concept successfully (Howell, 2000).

The range of HR tools which can be applied effectively in case of the various generations is important from the point of view of employer branding. Our results reveal that the most important driver for generation Z is still a high salary, although promotion opportunities and the promise of a good team, good atmosphere also came close to the top. The results of the quantitative research are in accordance with the conclusions of the qualitative research, where during the discussions about how they select their workplace, the first factor mentioned by respondents was the payment as well, and the most frequently mentioned drivers also included a good working atmosphere, attractive environment, and a good team, where they feel good while performing their job.

The results of the qualitative analysis show that fringe benefits and more free time also serve as great motivational factors, being on top of the preference list. While these were also important in the quantitative research, they were not perceived as the most important ones.

A creative working environment and the opportunity to implement their own ideas seemed to be more important than a good cafeteria system (Table 6.1).

The opinion of experts also confirms the conclusions of our research that even though the salary is important for the younger generations, it is not enough to retain members of this generation at a certain workplace. The employer brand is becoming more and more important for them, and consequently, their desire to be proud of working for that particular company. A pleasant atmosphere and development

Table 6.1   Ranking of Proper Motivation Tools

TO WHAT EXTENT DO THE FOLLOWING FACTORS MOTIVATE YOU FOR A BETTER PERFORMANCE AT WORK?	AVERAGE
Higher salary	**3.64**
Opportunity for promotion at the workplace	**3.46**
Opportunity for a career abroad	2.60
Greater independence in decisions	3.08
More free time, less work	3.21
Opportunity to implement own ideas	3.25
To work in a good team	**3.47**
Opportunities to take part in training sessions, professional development courses	2.97
Other fringe benefits (cafeteria)	3.22
Modern, creative working environment	3.32

and career opportunities are also important, as well as the fact that they should enjoy their job. If they are satisfied with these factors, there is a chance that they might spend longer time at a workplace (Kissné, 2014).

6.4.4 The Ranking of Drivers Influencing the Selection of Workplace,
      According to the Surveyed Generation Z

An employer must be familiar with the factors which play an important role in the selection of workplaces, when potential employees are making up their minds, which job or work opportunity they should choose. It is not by chance that a number of practicing HR experts believe that today an HR expert has to be a good salesman as well; they have to sell the announced position to make the workplace appealing both for the people who work there and for those who they are seeking to hire.

In order for an employer to be able to create such conditions at the workplace and to determine such an incentive package which is attractive for the candidates they are actually attempting to recruit, they must understand their expectations, values, and the range of factors these people consider when selecting their workplace. According to HR experts, the high level of motivation of employees might take a company to the top, if those people feel appreciated and see that their personal opinions, ideas, performance, and development actually contribute to the advancement of the company; if they can address the top leaders with their problems, because employees and the management speak the same language; if the company feels like their own, and they are proud to have a desk there (X), to work as one team (Y), and the company collects waste selectively and takes care of the environment (Z). The reason does not matter, they just want to be proud of the company (Kissné, 2014).

A research conducted in 1999 already revealed that employers have to face something new, an altered set of preferences when it comes to motivation at the workplace. According to the survey, employees can be best driven by (1) interesting work, (2) the recognition of the implemented work, and (3) the sense of being an insider. Only after that came (4) a secure workplace and (5) a good salary. The opportunity for development was the sixth on the list, and it was followed on the seventh place by good working conditions. These results were surprising since leaders expected the factors of good salary, a secure workplace, the opportunity for promotion/development, and interesting work to be on the top of the list (Kovach, 1999).

According to the Best Workplace 2012 research, respondents were seeking a (1) secure livelihood, (2) constant development and (3) diverse, interesting tasks at the ideal workplace, but almost every fourth respondent listed (4) professional challenges and (5) the opportunity for flexible work to be one of the top three most important factors. About 70% of them desires to work at a place where (6) they are appreciated financially and morally as well, and also more than 30% listed among the priorities that (7) the company should be steady and reliable, where they can (8) work in a good team, in a pleasant atmosphere.

Besides the factors which are important for everyone – such as a secure livelihood, stability, good working conditions – other attributes including social reputation, usefulness, helping others, cooperation with clients, controlling others, and development also became important for employees; nevertheless, social responsibility, the protection of the environment, and the mood of an employee while working in a company are factors gaining more and more attention (Boyett and Boyett, 2000; Kissné, 2010). According to the results of our quantitative research, when considering which job or workplace to choose, one of the major decisive factors is the opportunity for a promotion and professional development. It is esteemed even higher than a high salary for generation Z. The ranking of factors which play a role in the selection of a workplace looks quite similar to the range of efficient motivational tools.

It seems obvious that for this generation, offering a high salary and a good cafeteria, fringe benefits is not enough, as they are seeking for a company where they can realize their dreams, where they can fulfil a great and successful career path, and where they can work in a good team and atmosphere. The understanding of these aspects is important, because it clearly demonstrates the conditions a workplace should offer, the fields it should improve in order to appeal to the young generation, and to be able to retain its workforce.

Today, it poses an ever-increasing challenge for employers. Unlike earlier days, foreign ownership, the "multinational" characteristic

Table 6.2   Ranking of Factors Influencing the Selection of Workplace

FACTORS INFLUENCING THE SELECTION OF WORKPLACE	AVERAGE
The financial background of the company and the stability of its position on the market	3.40
The reputation and general perception of the company	3.07
Opportunities for promotion at the company	**3.49**
Proper work-life balance	3.40
Opportunity for working abroad	2.44
Other allowances and benefits besides the salary	3.13
Foreign ownership of the company	1.83
Predictable, fixed working hours	2.99
Opportunity for professional development	**3.48**
Diverse scope of duties	3.24
Creative tasks	3.17
Career opportunity	3.44
Company employing many people	2.13
High salary	**3.47**
Opportunity for continuing training and education	3.12
Good team spirit	**3.47**
Implementation of corporate social responsibility by the company	2.90
Company with a national reputation	2.31
Low average age of employees	2.43
Hungarian ownership	1.99
Multinational company	2.06
Employment by the company, and not through a work agency	3.25
Flexible working hours	3.02
Modern working environment	3.24
The distance of the workplace from home	3.23

of a company, is not an attractive factor for young people while selecting their workplace (Table 6.2). It is also important to note that compared to predictable and fixed working hours, the desire to fulfil a diverse scope of duties and to receive creative tasks seems even more significant. A modern working environment, meaning shorter traveling distance to the workplace and flexible working hours – similar to the results of our qualitative research – are significant aspects for this generation, even greater than the awareness and reputation of the company. It is good news for small- and medium-sized enterprises, who are able to offer more attractive opportunities in these fields, compared to the multinational corporations applying standard elements, who are less flexible in a number of aspects.

Table 6.3 The Most Attractive Factors

Which factors make a workplace attractive and ideal the most? (Mentions, in %, relative frequency, multiple answers were accepted)	
If it has a good reputation	32%
If employees are paid well	89%
If it is recommended by my friends, relatives	32%
If the workplace is trustworthy	80%
If there are good career opportunities	65%

When we asked respondents to select the top three factors which make a workplace appealing and ideal for them out of all the factors mentioned in Table 6.2, the most frequent mentions included (relative frequency, multiple answers were accepted) good salary, reliability, and good career opportunity. The reputation of the company and the opinion of friends and relatives were also important factors. The latter factor could be quite important for employer branding since it reveals the importance of what others say about a particular workplace and how employees feel about it.

Furthermore, it is definitely true in the aspect of employer branding that a credible communication and credible reputation is built from the inside. The opinion of employees influences the judgement of potential employees. The role of word-of-mouth and social channels are also just as significant for building the brand of an employer as in the case of building a consumer brand since consumer-generated marketing (CGM) generates the same effects here (Table 6.3).

6.5 Conclusion and Recommendations

Today, when a workplace has a hard time offering a single, good solution for the various generations, it is extremely important to understand the differentiated needs of these generations. In our study, we have focused on generation Z, and throughout our research, within the frame of a quantitative survey, we have attempted to find the answer to the question, what makes a workplace appealing for the Z's, and what are the most effective incentives at a workplace for them. A successful career path, a good working atmosphere and team spirit, and a good salary are the most important drivers during the selection of a workplace.

In case of those who already work there, a high salary and promotional opportunities serve as the best incentive. A workplace is considered to be ideal if employees are paid well, and if the company has the reputation of a reliable employer.

The results of the research revealed that the major milestones of an employer branding strategy focusing on generation Z are flexible HR, a diverse and interesting scope of duties and tasks, opportunities promising a higher status, greater financial benefits, and a responsible corporate behavior. Considering the fact that the opinion of friends and relatives is an important attribute of an ideal workplace, it is also essential to focus on the internal target group of employer branding during the course of communication since employees will become opinion leaders, ambassadors, those friends and relatives who actively shape the opinion of future potential employees. We believe that all of this requires a two-way, active communication from HR, and those who already work for the company must be reassured that they represent an active contribution to the reputation of the company. Results of the research also concluded that for generation Z, the nature of the corporate ownership (multinational, domestic) and the size of the company (a lot of or a few employees) do not matter, they are much more driven by a diverse scope of duties, team spirit, and career opportunities. It creates a great opportunity for small- and medium-sized enterprises to become an attractive workplace for youngsters since not only multinational companies, "the big ones" have the opportunity to design individual career paths, mentoring plans, or the creation of a good team spirit. In many cases, it might be implemented easier at a workplace with a lower number of staff.

References

Ali, B., Szikora, P. (2017). Az Y generáció és az internet kapcsolata. *Vállalkozásfejlesztés a XXI. században VII. Tanulmánykötet*, pp. 11–24.
Boyett, H.J., Boyett, J.T. (2000). World-class advice on managing and motivating people. Retrieved from: http://www.jboyett.com/managing1.htm. (Access: 9.11.2019).
Garda, I. (2009). *A motiváció elméletei*. Retrieved from: http://mlmhogyan.com/pszichologia/a-motivacio-elmeletei/. (Access: 05.10.2013).
Gonda, N. (2013). *Különböző generációk motivációs eszközeinek vizsgálata*. Budapest: OTDK Dolgozat.

Göndör, A. (2003). *Szervezeti viselkedés*. Budapest: Kézirat gyanánt.

Howell, H. (2000). *Motivating and appreciating your staff.* Retrieved from: http://v-p-c.com/catanzaro/mgtinfo/newsletter/spring2000/motivat. htm. (Access: 20.10.2019).

Kissné, A.K. (2010). *Hogyan motiválhatóak a különböző generációk tagjai?* Retrieved from: https://www.hrportal.hu/hr/hogyan-motivalhatoak-a-kulonbozo-generaciok-tagjai-20100804.html. (Access: 12.11.2019).

Kissné, A.K. (2014). *Lehet-e egységesen motiválni a különböző generációs munkaerőt?* Retrieved from: https://www.hrportal.hu/hr/lehet-e-egysegesen-motivalni-a-kulonbozo-generacios-munkaerot. (Access: 12.11.2019).

Klein, B., Klein, S. (2008). A motiváció. *Humánpolitikai Szemle, Év 19, Évf. 7-8*, pp. 31–57.

Kópházi, A.K. (2007). A motiváció szerepe a munkavállalói lojalitás megteremtésében. *Humánpolitikai Szemle, Év 18, Évf. 4*, pp. 51–56.

Kovach, K. (1999). *Employee motivation: Addressing a crucial factor in your organization's performance.* Ann Arbor, MI: University of Michigan Press.

Pink, D.H. (2010). *Motiváció 3.0. Ösztönzés másképp.* Budapest: HVG Kiadó Zrt,.

Ridderstrale, J.N. (2004). *Karaoke Kapitalizmus- Az emberiség menedzsmentje.* Kiadó: Wolters Kluwer Kft.

Tari, A. (2010). *Y generáció – Klinikai pszichológiai jelenségek és társadalomlélektani összefüggések az információs korban.* Budapest: Jaffa Kiadó.

Tari, A. (2011). *Z generáció.* Budapest: Tercium Könyvkiadó.

Törőcsik, M. (2003). *Fogyasztói magatartás – Trendek.* Budapest: KJK.

Tóth, J. (2009). *Személyiségpszichológia.* Retrieved from: http://mlmhogyan.com/pszichologia/tag/skinner/. (Access: 10.12.2019).

Tóthné, S.G. (2004). *Humán erőforrások gazdaságtana.* Miskolc: Bíbor Kiadó.

7

MODELS OF RESPONSIBLE BUSINESS: CSR FROM SOCIAL AND ECONOMIC PERSPECTIVE

MARCIN RATAJCZAK

Contents

7.1 Introduction

The first mentions of corporate social responsibility (CSR) date back to the turn of the 19th and 20th centuries and are closely linked to the philanthropic activities of large industrial tycoons (then corporations). One of such tycoons was Andrew Carnegie, who is considered as a precursor of CSR, primarily due to his considerations contained in the publication "The Gospel of Wealth" published in 1889 (Carnegie, 2012). His views were based on two principles: mercy and power. According to him, the principle of mercy requires happier members of society to support those less fortunate, including the unemployed, the disabled, the sick, and the elderly. In the case of the rule of ownership, the property of the entity was perceived as the property of the whole society entrusted to organizations for proper disposal, while enterprises should use it in a manner consistent with generally accepted social norms, that is, use only for purposes recognized by the society as legitimate (Stoner et al., 1999).

It is worth emphasizing that the development of the concept of responsible business had a great impact on the creation of agency theory in the 1930s by R. Coase (Jensen and Meckling, 1976). It implies the obligation of the so-called agent, who is a manager, another employee of the enterprise or an adviser, toward the principal, who in turn may be the owner or a senior manager. In this case, the goals of the agent and the principal can often be in a conflict of interest, for example, an employee expects more pay and the manager expects a higher profit for the organization (Fama, 1980). Therefore, a risk-sharing problem arises when the agent and principal have different views on decision-making and risk regarding the implementation of the task entrusted to them (Wołoszyn, et al., 2012). The business entity should then seek to multiply profits as expected by shareholders, and also invest in human capital, ensuring the professional development of all its employees (Crane et al., 2008).

Taking into account the historical approach to the concept of social responsibility discussed, it is certainly possible to consider the beginning of the definition approach by the publication of H. Bowen's book entitled *Social Responsibilities of the Businessman* in 1953 that is entirely devoted to these issues (Bowen, 1953). Through this publication, the author has clearly influenced the broader discussion about the responsibility associated with economic activity to such a level that Drucker (1998) began to wonder if American businessmen still have time to do business in their enterprises or they just deal with analyzing issues related to CSR. In his book, Bowen draws attention above all to the fact that all business decisions always have a direct impact on the lives of people in the society. This impact applies just to businessmen, shareholders, employees, clients, suppliers, or contractors in a direct and indirect way (Rogowski, 2016).

The main objective of this chapter is to present selected definitions of the CSR concept and to show responsible business models in terms of their implementation at the enterprise level.

Detailed objectives of the paper include the following:

• Characteristics and evaluation of selected models of social responsibility in a social context.
• Characteristics and assessment of selected CSR models in the economic aspect.

7.2 Selected CSR Definitions in the Light of the Literature

Considering the thorough analysis of the literature, attention should be paid to the variety of definitions presented, which is mainly due to the authors' willingness to take into account its various aspects, such as social, economic, political, ethical, moral, or environmental. Other definitive approaches are also influenced by economic systems dominating in a given country, the law in force and determining permissible activities in the sphere of business activity, and the political situation prevailing in a given period determining the ethical level of enterprises.

As mentioned before, the first definition of CSR is considered to be Bowen's proposal from 1953 – social responsibility is the responsibility of every businessman to pursue such policy, make such decisions, and strive for such actions that are desirable from the point of view of the set goals and social values (Bowen, 1953).

In the CSR definitions created in the 1960s, attention was paid mainly to the fact that the owner of an enterprise should predict the operation of the economic system and try to create close relations between the society and the organization for which he is to be responsible (Frederick, 1960; Walton, 1967).

The 1970s brought a very diverse approach to the definition of responsible business. On the one hand, the issues of profit and long-term business benefits were emphasized (Friedman, 1970; Ostlund, 1977), and on the other hand, attention was drawn to the need to increase the level of enterprise behavior to a level consistent with applicable standards, social values, and activities (Carroll, 1979; Davis, 1973; Sethi, 1975).

In the 1980s and 1990s, issues related to the role of stakeholder theory in the aspect of CSR, that is, employees, consumers, competitors, media, journalists, suppliers, government, associations, consumers, local communities, and business societies became key (Freeman, 1984), as well as a multidimensional approach to this concept, which makes it possible to combine the relationship between the principles of its implementation, a process based on social reactivity, as well as the organization's policy and action plan designed to manage social issues (Wartick and Cochran, 1985).

In turn, after 2000, the concept of CSR began to be understood as activities that support social good and are expected to go beyond the interests of the company and legal obligations (Williams and Siegel, 2000); as striving to generate profit, comply with the law, ethical behavior, and acting as a "good citizen" in relation to stakeholders (Hemphill, 2004). The CSR concept takes into account four basic goals of enterprises: focusing on obtaining long-term profits, conducting business in a responsible manner, taking into account the expectations of society and contributing to the good of society through ethically correct actions (Garriga and Mele, 2004), and is a dynamic and intensively considered concept, embedded in social, political, economic, and institutional context (Crane et al., 2008; Valor, 2005).

Weber (2011) stated in this period that the realization of profit of the enterprise should take into account the interests of all stakeholders. CSR models should be selected so that they maximize both business and social benefits.

Contemporary approaches to social responsibility indicate above all the connection between the implementation of the CSR concept in the network aspect and using modern IT tools, as well as using social media, and propose that it is implemented at the social level, that is, employed people and all directly related stakeholders (Hoivik and Shankar, 2011; Kim, 2017; Pana, 2013).

7.3 Models of Responsible Business in a Social Context

Various attempts are being made to model the concept of CSR in order to facilitate the practical implementation of its theoretical assumptions. One of the models assuming moral values first, and only then social and economic, is the *before profit obligation* model developed by Kang and Wood (1995). In this model, the key element is the moral responsibility of individual people (owners, employees, customers, and other stakeholders) in terms of ethical behavior and choices. They should all be guided by ethical and social norms generally applicable in a given economic system. At the second organizational level, only companies that meet social expectations of a moral nature and are practically feasible (taking into account the needs and expectations of stakeholders) deserve to function. Only the last level shows the economic aspect of the organization – if an economic entity contributes to the preservation and strengthening of social and economic order (implemented at the above-mentioned levels), then it has the right to generate income and profit.

A very interesting model approach to social responsibility was created by Davis (1975). This model contains five suggestions on how enterprises should behave in order to realistically implement the concept of responsible business in their activities and at the same time effectively take actions that bring economic, ethical, and ecological benefits to the whole society. Davis mainly indicates that social responsibility must always take into account the elements of impact on the whole society, that is, all stakeholders and the organization should implement this in two directions, creating an open system. When making key decisions related to launching production or services, social benefits and costs must always be analyzed in a wide scope and at least in part they should be borne by the consumers (clients) themselves.

It is also important that in addition to the basic scope of activity, every economic operator must engage in additional activities if it wants to be considered a responsible company. All proposals presented by Davis (1975) in the above model are connected to some extent. Due to the fact that enterprises have a very strong impact on the environment or employment structure, they should carefully analyze social expectations and contribute to raising the level of social well-being.

Due to the need for enterprises to design and implement social input strategies, models have also been created that determine socially responsible behavior of business entities.

The most common proposals in this area include models of Wartick and Cochran (1985) as well as Wood (1991). The first model assumes focusing on the company's social contract as a "good citizen" and identifying the social problems that arise, analyzing them and preventing them from arising. The organization should also minimize unexpected activities and create social policy with the highest efficiency, mainly at the economic entity level.

In turn, Wood (1991) in his model assumes implementation of the principles of social responsibility at the individual level (ethical decisions of the manager), organizational level (responsibility toward stakeholders), and the institutional level, that is, legal obligations and sanctions. He proposes to achieve social influence in the area of the organization's operation, to create social programs in cooperation with all stakeholders, and to integrate the developed social policy system with the strategy of the entire organization.

In the case of the rules proposed in both models, we can see clear differences. The Carroll pyramid was used in the Wartick and Cochran (1985) model – the authors of the model treated this model as principles and also recognized that the economic issue is fundamental, and only then the economic entity should strive to achieve other aspects of its activity. In implementing these principles, owners should be guided by the philosophy of the organization and remember to fulfill the role of a "good citizen." In turn, Wood (1991) indicates that the organization should be guided by three key principles, except that the first one applies to individuals making decisions and actions, which are treated as its moral agents and at the same time affecting the whole society (Karpacz, 2017).

At the level of social reaction processes itself, some similarities can be seen in these models. They assume that management on behalf of stakeholders, taking into account their needs and expectations, should be oriented toward shaping a social policy adequate to changes in the environment, and the ability to predict and prevent emerging social problems. In addition, Wood (1991) also indicates aspects of the assessment and monitoring of the state of the environment in his model that takes into account the environmental conditions of the organization.

It seems that it is worth mentioning the 3C-SR model developed by Meehan et al. (2006). It consists of three key elements, into which the authors include the so-called social sources (SR):

- Ethical and social commitments of the enterprise (commitments).
- Relations with business stakeholders forming a network of values (connections).
- Timeless consistency in confidence building (consistency).

The basic assumption of this model is fulfillment by the enterprise of all three elements called social sources. Obligations mean formal provisions that will be binding in the organization (ethical codes or accepted standards), and in this way, they will create the image of a socially responsible enterprise, with the assumption of compliance and respect, of course. In turn, relationships relate to the need to build effective business connections with all of the company's stakeholders, that is, employees, clients, contractors, and suppliers, by developing common social or economic solutions. In connection with these activities, consistency in their planning, implementation, and improvement is very important; this is exactly what confirms the credibility of undertaken activities and submitted declarations (Meehan et al., 2006).

The *LBG – the London Benchmarking Group* model – is one of the most proven management methodologies in the world of management, measuring and reporting the effectiveness of corporate social involvement. On February 9, 2011, the official inauguration of the LBG Polska network took place. The LBG methodology was developed in 1994 in the United Kingdom on the initiative of the Corporate Citizenship consultancy organization in cooperation with a group of companies that wanted to have access to a practical approach and tools to increase the efficiency of managing business social activities (LBG Guidance manual, 2014).

Globally, this model is currently used by over 300 companies, among others Vodafone, Unilever, Adidas, Coca-Cola, Heineken, GSK, 3M, Deloitte, PwC, IBM, Intel, Toyota, Skanska, Aviva, Axa, and many more. All these companies recognize the benefits of implementing this model to the full extent. The LBG model allows an accurate and comprehensive calculation of the value of the overall social commitment of the organization, thus expressing in monetary terms the total costs that the company incurs in connection with the implementation of socially responsible activities (LBG Guidance manual, 2014).

7.4 CSR Models in the Economic Context

One of the most popular and at the same time the most commonly used models indicating the economic aspect of socially responsible activities is the Carroll (1999) model, called *after profit obligation.*

It implies that CSR activities occur on four planes (or levels): philanthropic (desired by society), ethical (socially expected), legal, and economic (required by society).

According to the assumptions of the above model, the economic aspect is a key aspect of the company's operations. First of all, the organization should be profitable, or at least not generate financial losses. At the second level of this model there is legal responsibility, that is, the organization must always comply with the law in force in a given country, mainly economic. Moreover, it is the organization's responsibility to comply with this law when operating in an ever-changing market and in strong competition (Carroll, 1999).

At the third level, ethical responsibility, the issue of entity ethics, that is, managers in enterprises and at the same time persons responsible for the decisions and actions of the organization, is clearly emphasized. The key aspects at this level are the ethical climate around the company, as well as formal documents present in the organization, for example, ethical codes or CSR strategies. The last level is philanthropy, which takes into account the various activities of the entire entity and individual employees to improve living conditions in a broad sense or to solve existing social problems. It is worth noting that the CSR hierarchy developed by Carroll (1999) gives an intuitive sense to many ways of describing a set of managerial responsibilities in the field of broadly understood CSR.

On the other hand, Werther and Chandler (2006) in their model approach, pay attention primarily to the economic element, that is, the implementation of CSR principles allows to gain a competitive advantage and is an important distinguishing feature of the organization in the event of avoiding possible penalties for noncompliance with ethical principles in its functioning. It is worth emphasizing that in their assumptions they also take into account moral issues (whether the company can grow independently without the presence of society) and rational (the organization's activities must be implemented in accordance with the law).

An interesting model approach is presented by Matten (2006), who distinguishes three perspectives in the context of responsible business. The most important of them is the economic perspective; it includes the company's activities emphasizing the responsibility of the board for creating products and services that will ensure high sales in the long run, and thus achievement of profit. In addition to the above perspective, the author also points to social issues (expectations and needs of stakeholders) and environmental protection, through the skillful use of natural resources due to understanding the problem of their limitedness.

Finally, it is worth mentioning the three-domain CSR model that was developed by Schwartz and Carroll (2003). In the already mentioned fields, the authors included economic, legal, and ethical. Within the economic field (recognized as key in this model), activities are included to obtain a positive economic impact in a given business entity, for example, by increasing sales or acquiring new customers. The need to take actions that affect the company's profit or improve its image in the market is clearly emphasized.

In turn, the legal field refers to the responsibility of the organization in the aspect of legal requirements oriented and expected by a given community, mainly local. The last field, ethical, aims to promote behaviors expected by generally applicable standards, as well as the immediate environment of the company (Schwartz and Carroll, 2003).

7.5 Conclusion

Summing up the above considerations, it can be stated that all presented models of responsible business are certainly of great importance in making the final decision by enterprises to implement the concept of CSR in practice. To a large extent, it depends on what in a particular economic entity will be considered a key activity – whether economic, social, or ecological aspect.

It is worth emphasizing that clear and transparent ethical principles, implementation as part of CSR modeling approaches, are very important primarily in relations with employees. It is in this aspect that they show a clear framework of conduct, focusing on the activities accepted by the organization and those considered unethical. Thanks to this approach, the employee can be sure that he or she makes the right decisions based on the assumptions of the responsible business model, which has been accepted and implemented in practice by the business entity.

In addition to the above, it should also be stated that social responsibility in the model context must be taken into account in the activities inside and outside each enterprise. It must be treated as the foundation of business, not as additional ethical activities undertaken in selected areas and activities of the organization. Comprehensive activities undertaken by business entities and having a coherent value system are the basic elements of stable and proper functioning in the market. Such actions will definitely avoid many risks and costs resulting from unethical behavior or incorrect business decisions.

Review of the most important CSR models showed their high heterogeneity. In some, the focus is clear on social aspects, in others, economic elements are key. This is due to the fact that in the former, the role of stakeholders (including the community) in the development of the enterprise and thus their influence on the functioning of the organization in the market is clearly emphasized. On the other hand, economic issues in CSR models relate mainly to increasing efficiency, which translates into economic added value for all key stakeholders. This approach will definitely be possible to be achieved by conscious managers who will be able to orient the organization's activities toward creating high economic value, while remembering about the basic ethical principles in force in a given industry.

At the end of the discussion, it can be stated that CSR should not be treated only as costs that enterprises cannot afford, but above all social and economic benefits for their owners and stakeholders, as well as a positive impact on the environment. Entrepreneurs very often do not have such awareness, which is why it seems reasonable to promote all model activities in this field and emphasize the growing importance of the aspect of social responsibility in business practice, both on the domestic and foreign market.

The limitations of research in the field of CSR models include the lack of a unified tool that would allow comparison of analysis results. There is a very wide variety of measurement methods, research techniques, and indicators used to analyze and evaluate socially responsible business models. This study is a contribution to determining the scale of validity of the proposed CSR models in the context of their implementation in economic entities, emphasizing the economic and social element. Development of a model approach should be indicated as the directions of future research in this field, which would give the opportunity to implement this concept not only in economic but also in social, ecological, and ethical aspects.

References

Bowen, H. (1953). *The social responsibilities of businessman.* New York: Harper & Row.

Carnegie, A. (2012). *Ewangelia bogactwa. The Gospel of Wealth.* Tłumaczenie H. Górnicka-Holeczek. Poznań: Wydawnictwo M-Serwis M. Bukowian i inni.

Carroll, A. (1979). A three dimensional conceptual model of corporate performance. *Academy of Management Review, 4(4),* pp. 497–505.

Carroll, A.B. (1999). Corporate social responsibility – Evolution of a definitional construct. *Business & Society, 38(3),* pp. 48–49.

Crane, A., Matten, D., Spence, L. (2008). Corporate social responsibility: In a global context. In: A. Crane, D. Matten, L. Spence (eds.), *Corporate social responsibility: Readings and cases in a global context.* Canada: Routledge, pp. 3–20

Davis, K. (1973). The case for and against business assumption of social responsibilities. *Academy of Management Journal, 16(2),* pp. 312–323.

Davis, K. (1975). Five propositions for social responsibility. *Business Horizons. EconPapers, 18(3),* pp. 19–23.

Drucker, P. (1998). *Praktyka zarządzania.* Kraków: Akademia Ekonomiczna.

Fama, E. (1980). Agency problems and the theory of the firm. *Journal of Political Economy, 88,* pp. 290–306.

Frederick, W. (1960). The growing concern over business responsibility. *California Management Review, 2,* pp. 54–61.

Freeman, E. (1984). *Strategic management: A stakeholder approach.* Boston: Pitman.

Friedman, M. (1970). The social responsibility of business is to increase its profits. *New York Times Magazine,* September.

Garriga, E., Mele, D. (2004). Corporate social responsibility theories: Mapping the territory. *Journal of Business Ethics, 53,* pp. 51–74.

Hemphill, T. (2004). Corporate citizenship: The case for a new corporate governance model. *Business & Society Review, 109(3),* pp. 339–361.

Hoivik, H.W., Shankar, D. (2011). How can SMEs in a cluster respond to global demands for corporate responsibility? *Journal of Business Ethics, 101(2),* pp. 175–195.

Jensen, M.C., Meckling, W.H. (1976). Theory of the firm: Managerial behaviour, agency costs and ownership structure. *Journal of Financial Economics, 3,* pp. 306–355.

Kang, Y.Ch., Wood, D.J. (1995). Before profit social responsibility turning the economic paradigm upside down. In: D. Nigh, D. Collins, (eds.), *Proceedings of the 6th Annual Meeting of the International Association for Business and Society.* Vienna, Austria. pp. 408–418.

Karpacz, J. (2017). *Społeczna odpowiedzialność biznesu. Ewolucja definiowania konstruktu.* Studia Ekonomiczne Regionu Łódzkiego, Nr 24, pp. 144–145.

Kim, Y. (2017). Consumer responses to the food industry's proactive and passive environmental CSR, factoring in price as CSR tradeoff. *Journal of Business Ethics, 140(2),* pp. 307–321.

LBG Guidance manual. (2014). *From inputs to impact – Measuring corporate community contributions through the LBG framework*. London: Corporate Citizenship.

Matten, D. (2006). *Why do companies engage in corporate social responsibility? Background, reasons and basic concepts*. In: *The ICCA handbook on corporate social responsibility*. Chichester: John Wiley & Sons, pp. 3–46.

Meehan, J., Meehan, K., Richards, A. (2006). Corporate social responsibility: The 3C-SR model. *International Journal of Social Economics, 33(5)*, pp. 392–393.

Ostlund, L. (1977). Attitudes of managers toward corporate social responsibility. *California Management Review, 19(4)*, pp. 35–49.

Pana, L. (2013). Social efficacy by responsible change management. *Systemic Practice and Action Research, 26(6)*, pp. 579–588.

Rogowski, R. (2016). Praktyka wdrażania CSR w polskich przedsiębiorstwach w opinii doradców. *Annales. Etyka w życiu gospodarczym, 19(1)*, pp. 37–54.

Schwartz, M., Carroll, A. (2003). Corporate social responsibility: A three-domain approach. *Business Ethics Quarterly, 13*, pp. 508–511.

Sethi, S. (1975). Dimensions of corporate social performance. An analytic framework. *California Management Review, 17(3)*, pp. 58–64.

Stoner, J.A.F., Freeman, R.E., Gilbert, D.R. (1999). *Kierowanie*. Warszawa: Polskie Wydawnictwo Ekonomiczne,

Valor, C. (2005). Corporate social responsibility and corporate citizenship: Towards corporate accountability. *Business & Society Review, 110*, pp. 191–212.

Walton, C. (1967). *Corporate social responsibilities*. Belmont: Wadsworth Publishing Company Inc.

Wartick, S.L., Cochran. P.L. (1985). The evolution of the corporate social performance model. *Academy of Management Review, 10(4)*, pp. 758–769.

Weber, M. (2011). *Racjonalność, władza, odczarowanie*., Poznań: Wydawnictwo Poznańskie.

Werther, W.B., Chandler, D. (2006). *Strategic corporate social responsibility: Stakeholders in a global environment*. Thousand Oaks: Sage Publications,

Williams, A., Siegel, D. (2000). Corporate social responsibility and financial performance: Correlation or misspecification? *Strategic Management Journal, 21(5)*, pp. 603–609.

Wołoszyn, J., Stawicka, E., Ratajczak, M. (2012). *Społeczna odpowiedzialność małych i średnich przedsiębiorstw agrobiznesu z obszarów wiejskich*. Warszawa: Wydawnictwo SGGW

Wood, D.J. (1991). Corporate social performance revisited. *Academy of Management Review, 16*, pp. 691–718.

8

CYBER PROTECTION: INDUSTRIALIZED ASSESSMENTS FOR ANALYZING CYBER RISK

DAVID NICOLAS BARTOLINI, CÉSAR BENAVENTE-PECES, AND ANDREAS AHRENS

Contents

8.1 Introduction

Cyber risks often cause unknown financial damage to companies. Technical progress of information systems leading to interconnection of systems, data storage in databases (DDBB) and sharing, and complex technology architectures are increasing the risks of cyber exposure. Cyber risks primarily affect digital information security. Cyber risk can jeopardize the availability, integrity, and confidentiality of sensitive data, processes, and information when they are realized. The success of new technologies and services on line and on the cloud, such as cloud computing or the Internet of Things, has pushed cyber risk into the realm of general risk perception, especially as more and more end customers are affected by risk exposure. Compared to traditional risks, however, cyber risks are still a relatively new threat to companies, especially for small ones. Cyber Incidents and massive data breaches at several companies have gained a strong presence in scientific and research community, and media, especially in recent years, due to the accumulation of incidents. An example of this fact is the recent hacker attack on British Airways, which resulted in the disclosure of sensitive customer information. For insurance companies offering cyber protection to their customers, this is a major challenge. Insurance companies rely on data that have been stored for decades in private liability insurance or in motor vehicles to evaluate their risk. Since this is not the case in the context of cyber risks, their own underwriters work together with technical IT security experts to evaluate the respective customer situation. This takes place within a multi-tier process and includes a risk dialogue (Bartolini et al., 2017), a questionnaire-based approach (Bartolini et al., 2018) for evaluating the cyber risks and a macroeconomic assessment of the client including the client's branch. This chapter is aimed at showing how this macroeconomic assessment can be carried out by means of a novel approach based on machine learning (ML). The remaining part of this chapter is structured as follows: In Section 2, the general approach is introduced. In Section 3, several ML algorithms and their results will be described. In Section 4, the models will be compared, and a final evaluation proceeded. Finally, some concluding remarks are provided in Section 5.

8.2 Evaluation of Technical and Business Risk Features for a Machine Learning Approach

Business Intelligence (BI) focuses on the independent analysis of data (Rud, 2009). This feature is aimed at predicting the outcome of a business strategy, which in the context of an insurance in terms of risk management is the selection of customer-specific factors. Therefore, the economic risk assessment first requires this data. BI is a good concept for insurance companies to use information in an intelligent way. Here, the results of strategies are based on the data analysis. On the other hand, ML works in a different way. Its functionality is more focused on understanding the system itself (Bishop, 2006). Therefore, both are complementary and needed by an insurance company to make an underwriting decision. ML focuses on learning patterns by accessing the collected data available in the system databases and transforming that data into information and decision, which is the main concern of the investigation introduced in this chapter.

Since there are no databases with Cyber Incidents and loss data etc. available on which insurance companies base their risk management, at least Cyber Insurance specialized insurance companies can use their own data to work out evaluations and features for ML. We selected such an available dataset to develop a Cyber Insurance ML claims prediction model. In doing so, features must be appropriately selected to make them helpful to better assess the cyber risk, that is, to predict a possible occurrence of claims. The approach chosen will explore which factors play a significant role in insurers' economic risk assessment. Following feature selection criteria have been applied for this approach:

- *Turnover of the insured company.* The greater the company's Turnover, the greater its size and thus its IT infrastructure. In addition, a large and well-known company is more exposed to a cyber attack than a small one.
- *Other IT insurances.* For an economic as well as a risk-based approach, it is a relevant aspect if the company has more IT insurances besides the Cyber Insurance and if this additional risk transfer has a positive correlation.
- *Credit card/cardholder and personal identifying information (CC/ PII) data.* Data breaches have dramatic outcomes in which

personal data as well as cardholder data are stolen by criminals. Claims payments can arise when the company is forced to pay fines in the legal context (e.g., General Data Protection Regulation, 2016) or in the regulatory context (e.g., PCI Security Standards Council, 2018).

- *The result of the technical cyber risk assessment.* As described in related work (Bartolini et al., 2018), a company can be technically insured if the result of the cyber risk assessment (technical risk assessment) reaches minimum 2.00 Rating. Therefore, this criterion is also relevant for the approach.
- *The customer is one of the critical infrastructures.* As critical infrastructures are a high target for criminals, these companies need to have a high maturity level.
- *Investments in IT/Cyber Programs*, another economic figure for correlation analysis. In general, it seems high development in this area will be a positive risk factor.
- *Cyber damage has finally occurred.* The factor if a Cyber Insurance claim has already occurred at the company is a very important aspect for the approach.

For better illustration of the seven described features, we have extracted the first five datasets and visualized these features in the figures of Table 8.1.

The total number of insured company's dataset includes 1,295 customers. The seven features (Table 8.2, Figure 8.1a–8.1f) of the ML approach will be described next. In total, 758 customers already raised an insurance claim, while for 537 this was not the case (Table 8.2). The annual Turnover of the insured companies varies widely. There are only a few companies with a Turnover exceeding 100M EUR.

Table 8.1   Relevant Features Affecting Insurability

	Turnover	Other IT Insurance	CC / PII	Rating	KRITIS	Cyber Invest	Insurance claim
0	19	0	27.90	3.0	1	1.688492e+07	1
1	18	1	33.77	3.0	0	1.725552e+03	1
2	28	1	33.06	3.0	0	4.449462e+06	0
3	33	1	22.70	3.0	0	2.198447e+04	0
4	32	1	28.88	3.0	0	3.866855e+03	1

Table 8.2 Dataset Features. Insurance Claim

Companies experienced minimum one Cyber Insurance Claim	758
Companies without any Cyber Insurance Claims	537

However, most companies have a Turnover significantly below 60M EUR per year (Figure 8.1a). As explained in the authors' previous work (Bartolini et al., 2018) on the Cyber Insurance Risk Assessment, a rating result must be at least 2.00 for a company to be eligible for Cyber Insurance. This is also reflected in Figure 8.1b as no data less than 2.00 exists in the dataset. Most of the insured companies have been rated between 2.00 and 3.00 and only very few have a better rating. Next, sensitive data such as cardholder data or personal data are stored in most companies well below 10,000 records. But for some companies, the collection of these stored records is well over 50,000 (Figure 8.1c).

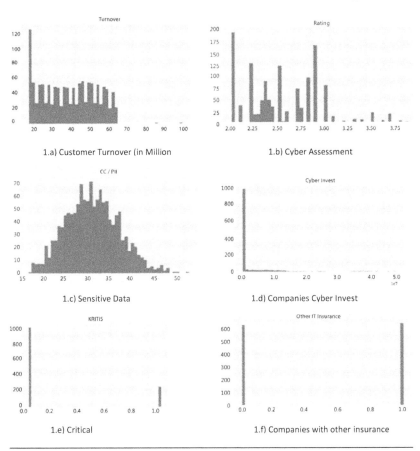

1.a) Customer Turnover (in Million

1.b) Cyber Assessment

1.c) Sensitive Data

1.d) Companies Cyber Invest

1.e) Critical

1.f) Companies with other insurance

Figure 8.1   Dataset features for the different parameters.

Especially in the context of regulatory and legal requirements, such a high amount of sensitive data is critical and in the context of a data protection violation, a huge number of potential customers are affected. Information regarding investments in cyber protection and programs moves up to 1M EUR per year for most companies.

Few companies invest more than 4M EUR a year (Figure 8.1d). The so-called critical infrastructures (KRITIS) were included in less than 300 companies among the dataset. One of the reasons for this is that certain risks are excluded from Insurance cover because their risk cannot be accepted. Finally, among the insured companies, the ratio is quite balanced, between those who use additional other IT insurance as protection against the cyber risk and those who only use the cyber insurance as a risk transfer measure.

Based on this data, it will be first relevant how the correlations of every pair of these variables (features) look like. As can be seen from the heatmap in Figure 8.2, there is a strong correlation between CC/PII and insurance claims as well as between KRITIS and Insurance claims.

Turnover also has a certain relevance, as well the Rating on Insurance claims. Although it can be stated that there is a certain

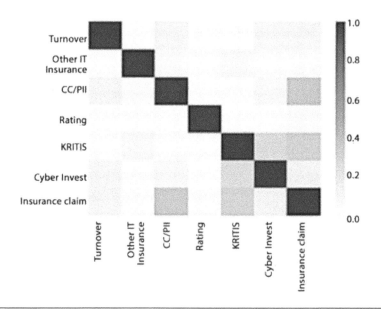

Figure 8.2   Heatmap. Correlation between features.

correlation between the investment in cyber security and KRITIS in companies, this fact generally has little significance for Insurance Claims. The same conclusion can in principle be interpreted for Other IT Insurance. As we want to predict target numeric values, then a supervised learning method must now be chosen. In this chapter, we will focus on the most relevant algorithms: Logistic Regression, Linear Regression, Random Forests, Gradient Boosted Trees, etc. The Python Scikit-Learn library is used for all these algorithms. In order to process the data collected in Scikit-Learn (2019) (as already shown in heatmap), it has to be binary. Therefore, One Hot Encoding is used. One way to evaluate a model is to split the training set into smaller training sets and evaluate against the validation set. Therefore, we use Scikit-Learn cross-validation, and our three sets for all models in this chapter are divided into training sets (containing 80% of the data), test set (10%), and the mentioned cross-validation set (10%). Cross-validation is used to reduce the problem of overfitting. The aim is to find out which algorithm is the best claims predictor.

8.3 Machine Learning Algorithms for Cyber Insurance Decision-Making Process

8.3.1 Analysis with Regression Algorithms

The goal of this procedure is to use a regression for every class and setting, the output equals 1 for training instances that belong to the class and 0 for those not belonging to that class (classification and clustering). The result is a linear output for the class. Next, if given test data of an unknown class, calculation of the value of each linear expression can be made and the best one can be chosen. This is often called multi-response linear regression (Breiman and Friedman, 1997). In the case of multi-response linear regression, it is observed that a fair membership is created for each class. With a new instance, it can be calculated for its membership to a class afterward and finally the best one selected. Besides the fact that multi-response linear regression often brings up good results, it has also some drawbacks. As some produced values can fall outside of the range of 0 and 1, least squares regression also assumes that errors are not only statistically independent but are also normally distributed with the same standard deviation.

In this investigation, we are looking for a regression algorithm as simple as possible, capable to provide relevant information so that we can make predictions about the dependent variable as better as possible. The target value and the input value have to be put in relation to each other. It should also be noted that some points cannot be perfectly described by a straight line and therefore not every error can be caught. At regression, therefore, it makes sense to use the root mean square error (RMSE) as a performance measure which gives information of how much error the system makes in its predictions. In the following sections, we compare first Linear Regression algorithm with each other and finalize with the Logistic Regression.

8.3.2 Linear Regression

This algorithm is the simplest and very popular on ML as it can be fit very quickly and is good to interpret as well (Yan, 2009). This helps us with our aim to predict the Insurance Claims closest to the actual claims data. A regression function describes the trend or the average relationship between numerical attributes. A Linear Regression assumes that there is a linear relationship between the data and the associated function values, that the relationship between the x and y values is linear, and that it can therefore be described by a straight line.

The aim is to minimize the error between the actual target value and the calculated value, so that positive and negative deviations do not compensate each other. In this context, the mean squared error is examined.

Linear Regression itself is prone to overfitting when basis function is used (Harrell, 2001). Such a behavior is a problem, and it would be better if there are possibilities to limit overfitting or to raise penalties for this behavior. At Linear Regressions, there are no parameters which can influence this. This is possible when regularization is used (Bühlmann and van de Geer, 2011). Therefore, we look at regularization in the following methods when we validated the best approach.

8.3.3 Ridge Regression (L2)

The Ridge Regression, also called L2 regression, is to regulate the Linear Regression algorithm while training (Tikhonov, 1963). The regularization can be controlled with a hyper parameter.

8.3.4 Lasso Regression (L1)

The only difference to the Ridge Regression is that Lasso uses the L1, which is the weighted vector (Santosa and Symes, 1989; Tibshirani, 1996), instead of the L2 algorithm to regularize the linear regression model.

In binary, we can decide if an Insurance Claim happened with a 1, or if there is no claim with a 0. Therefore, the threshold is at 0.5.

Regression model claim prediction

$$R = \begin{cases} 0 \ \textit{if} \ \varnothing(i) < 0.5 \\ 1 \ \textit{if} \ \varnothing(i) \geq 0.5 \end{cases} \tag{8.1}$$

First, a model was used without regularization, afterward one with Lasso regularization (L1), and finally one with Ridge regression (L2) using Scikit-Learn. After analyzing Figure 8.3a to 8.3c, we conclude that it shows a good performance just in the case where few instances of the fit training set are used (curve starts at 0), that is, as more datasets are added, it is found that there isn't any model that can appropriately fit in an acceptable way. The top of the error will be reached at a certain point, when adding more data to the training does not make any differences regarding the average error results. In contrast, the performance of the model is different with validation data. There is a big difference with only a few datasets at the beginning, which is why the curve starts much more clearly above 0. However, with increasing datasets each model learns and achieves that the validation error decreases. In the context of Cyber Insurance datasets, it has become clear that our Cyber Insurance dataset cannot be analyzed very well with an unregulated linear regression model.

This is made clear by the noticeably large RMSE (see Table 8.2). The regulation of the linear model by means of L1 and L2 makes sense in the first view, since RMSE could be significantly reduced. The best result was achieved with the Ridge Regression. However, an unrestricted further use of the model is not advisable. The present

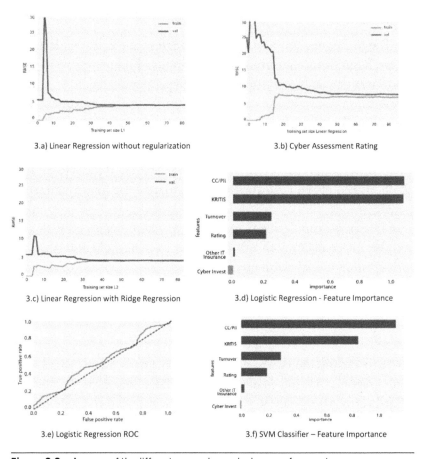

Figure 8.3 Accuracy of the different approaches and relevance of parameters.

dataset for Cyber Insurance cannot be separated linearly very well. This is much clearer by its properties in Figure 8.3c, where it can be seen that the error does not fall below a certain level and that this level is very close to the train set. Furthermore, it has to be stated that the model is underfitting. As long as a model is underfitting on the training set, a parameter control does not help, even adding further datasets does not (Burnham and Anderson, 2002). You can try to get more features, but the much more efficient approach is to choose a more complex model and algorithms (Table 8.3).

Table 8.3 Results of Algorithms

Linear	Lasso (L1)	Ridge (L2)
RMSE: 0.72	RMSE: 0.44	RMSE: 0.42

8.3.5 Analysis with Classification Algorithms

To further analyze the Cyber Insurance dataset, we now use another supervised learning approach – classification. Based on given examples, whose class affiliation is given, a classification of new datasets, whose class affiliation is unknown, is carried out. Classification methods are application-oriented, so that many different methods exist (Alpaydin, 2010).

8.3.6 Logistic Regression

Logistic Regression models perform very well on linearly separable classes. Therefore, it is one of the most used algorithms for classification. Despite its name, the logistic regression is a widely used binary classifier. As mentioned before, we need One Hot Encoding for calculation of ML algorithms for binary classifier. Any regression option, linear or not linear, can be used for classification. At Logistic Regressions, it can be figured out if an instance belongs to a class if the probability is greater than 50% (1) or not (0) with binaries. Finally, in logistic regression, a linear model is within a logistic function. Logistic Regression also uses L2 regularization, as Ridge does with regression. However, in Logistic Regression, the parameter is called C. Higher values for C mean less regularization.

To get a better understanding of what happened inside the Logistic Regression model, the visualization in Figure 8.3f shows how the model uses the different features and which of them have greater effects. The feature engineering process involves selecting the minimum required features to produce a valid model, because the more features a model contains, the more complex it is, therefore the more sensitive the model is to errors due to variance (Domingos, 2012). A common practice to eliminating features is to describe their relative importance to a model, then eliminate weak features or combinations of features, and re-evaluate to see if the model fairs better during cross-validation.

Regarding feature importance, the following conclusions can be made. First, CC/PII and KRITIS have significant influence on taking decisions. Not only hearing of data breaches and exposure of personal data and/or cardholder data in the news, the same experience will be made following the ML algorithm results. Second, Cyber Investments has a negative influence on the prediction. For instance, higher investments in cyber security are correlated with customers not taking Insurance Claims.

Next, we are looking at the practical implementation of the logistic regression algorithm in Python Scikit-Learn library. At the dataset, the label and features for both training and test datasets have been separated and input normalization has been performed. This helps understanding feature importance. By creating an instance and training the model with the fit function, the accuracy can be generated out of the test data. When adjusting C, different results can generally be obtained. At high C values, the algorithm tries to adjust the training data in the best possible way. Low C values, however, allow the model to find a coefficient vector that is close to 0 (Muller, 2017). We generated the best result with our model approach after adjusting C to 10,000. The best training data accuracy was achieved with 76% with the Logistic Regression algorithm.

To get an even better insight into the Cyber Insurance dataset, let us now introduce the receiver operating characteristic curve (ROC curve). By means of the ROC, the true positive rate is plotted in the context of the false positive rate. The false positive rate is the ratio of the negative instances which were wrongly classified as positive (Fawcett, 2006). In Figure 8.4a, the dotted line is a completely random classification. A good model should be as far away as possible from this line and as close to the upper left corner as possible. Therefore, we consider that for the Cyber Insurance datasets the Logistic Regression is not further considered, because this model is also underfitted.

8.3.7 Support Vector Machines

Support Vector Machines (SVMs) are powerful tools for classification. SVMs divide a set of objects into classes in such a way that the widest possible area around the class boundaries remains free of objects (Cortes and Vapnik, 1995). The starting point for building a SVM is the available set of training objects, for each of which it is known which class it belongs to. Each object is represented by a

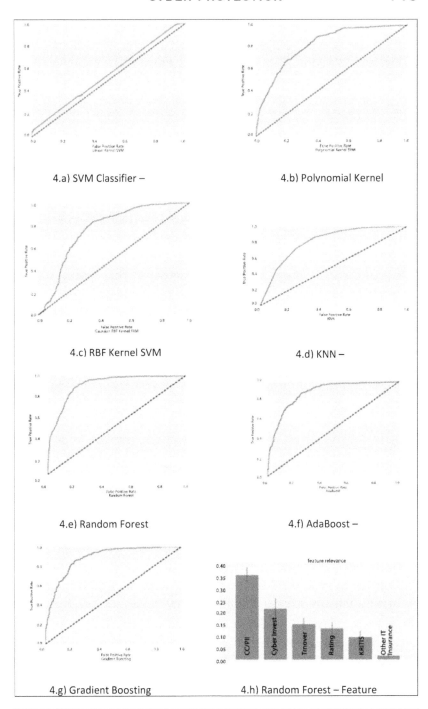

4.a) SVM Classifier –   4.b) Polynomial Kernel

4.c) RBF Kernel SVM   4.d) KNN –

4.e) Random Forest   4.f) AdaBoost –

4.g) Gradient Boosting   4.h) Random Forest – Feature

Figure 8.4   ROC for different approaches and relevance.

vector in a vector space. The task of the SVM is to fit a hyperplane into this space, which acts as a dividing surface and divides the training dataset into two classes. The distance between the vectors closest to the hyperplane is maximized (Raschka and Mirjalili, 2019). This wide, empty border will later ensure that even objects that do not correspond exactly to the training objects are classified as reliably as possible.

A vector is a straight line through the coordinate origin and hyperplanes run perpendicular to this straight line. Each intersects the line at a certain distance b from the origin measured in the opposite direction to the vector. This distance is called bias (Raschka and Mirjalili, 2019). Together, the vector and the bias uniquely determine a hyperplane.

For points that do not lie on the hyperplane, the value is not 0, but positive (on the side to which the vector is pointing to). If the hyperplane separates the two classes, then the sign for all points of one class is +1 and for all points of the other class is −1. In order to carry out the simplified binary classification, we define the classification function as a vector composed by two parts: the first one, called class +1, containing the elements whose value is greater than 0, and the second one, called class −1, containing the elements whose value is lower than 0.

Input vectors which can be separated by such a hyperplane are called linearly separable (Boyd and Vandenberghe, 2004). Hard margin is possible at clear linear separable data. But, as not every dataset is linearly separable and outliers are also common, therefore, there must be adjustments within the ML algorithm. At Scikit-Learn SVM classes, we are able to control the margin with the C hyper parameter – which is the same as it was described at Logistic Regression. Here, a lower C leads to a higher margin but with a lot of outliers. A higher C will lead to a lower margin but fewer outliers (Raschka and Mirjalili, 2019). It is important to select the correct kernel to fit the problem, because the vector space contains little relevant data if the kernel function is chosen badly (Cortes and Vapnik, 1995). By parameter optimization, the kernels can be further refined to find the optimal spaces. The different kernel methods and their parameters are described in more detail below.

8.3.8 Linear Kernel SVM Classification

First, we are looking at Linear Kernel SVM. This kernel method is the simplest kernel function and almost every library is pre-implemented. Using the algorithm on the dataset we are receiving after the adjustment on C parameter, the best results when C is set to 1.0. With this, we achieve an accuracy of 87% on our training dataset.

Now, we perform settings on our test dataset, and we achieve the Insurance Claim probability of 82% as the array [0.1774705, 0.8225295] leads to an Insurance Claim Prediction array [1]. That means that the dataset has an 18% chance of being class 0 and 82% chance of being class 1.

Next, regarding Feature Importance at Linear SVM Classifier (Figure 8.4b), the following conclusions can be made. First, CC/PII and KRITIS have significant influence as we saw it at Logistic Regression, and Cyber Investment has a negative influence on the prediction as well. But here we see the Rating as a higher importance than Turnover.

After we saw the model's accuracy, let us now have also a look at the ROC curve (Figure 8.4c). As mentioned before, a good model should be as far away from the dotted line and as close to the upper left corner as possible. It can be seen from the ROC curve that the linear SVM model is not very effective with the Cyber Insurance dataset as it was thought it would be regarding the achieved accuracy. Although the dotted line is not touched as it is the case with, for example, Logistic Regression, but the distance between the lines is not big enough. Therefore, we adjust the kernel by considering other SVM models.

Polynomial Kernel SVM

KNN Confusion Matrix ([[239, 141],
    [76, 494]])

The Polynomial Kernel is a frequently used kernel for SVM classification. It is especially suitable for problems where all training data has been normalized (Goldberg and Elhadad, 2008). It is implemented in many libraries like Scikit-Learn.

After applying this to the train datasets, we were able to get an accuracy of 100%. We used the poly kernel with the tree degree of 5. We made several adjustments to C parameters. Best results were obtained when choosing C equal 100. As the accuracy was perfect on the training set, we will compare the results with the next SVM algorithm, as in general the polynomial method is very computational expensive.

8.3.9 Gaussian RBF Kernel SVM

Although linear SVM classifiers are very efficient and work well in many cases, a lot of datasets are not being separable. Just as the polynomial feature method, the similarity feature method can be very interesting for ML algorithms. The main issue is the computational expensiveness of such a model. To get this problem under control, we can use the kernel trick with SVM. This has the same effect as if we were adding many similar features without doing it (Muller, 2012). The Radial Basis Function (RBF) Kernel, or Gaussian Kernel, is one of the most widely used kernel methods for SVM classification and is therefore implemented in many libraries (Chang et al., 2010). The choice of sigma plays a remarkable role in the performance of the kernel, because the kernel behaves like the Linear Kernel if the value is too high (Géron, 2017).

After applying this algorithm to the training dataset, we were able to get an accuracy of 100% as that we achieved with the polynomial kernel. We used the Gaussian RBF kernel of the Scikit-Learn Support Vector Classifier (SVC) class. We made several adjustments to the gamma and C parameters. Best results were obtained when choosing C equal to 100. Since we have not yet explained gamma, a short description is needed. The effect of gamma is like a regularization parameter. This means that if the model should be overfitting, then gamma should be reduced, and if it should be underfitting, then gamma should be increased (Raschka and Mirjalili, 2019). After implementing this approach on the dataset, the following results are obtained on the test dataset.

Insurance Claim Probability [0.1198319, 0.88051681] and Insurance Claim Prediction [1]. These results mean that the dataset has a 12% chance of being class 0 and 88% chance of being class 1. As expected, without any surprise our result is better than the one obtained with the Linear Kernel.

After showing the models accuracy, now the properties of the ROC curve (Figure 8.4b, Figure 8.4c) are analyzed. As already mentioned before, a good model should be as far away from the dotted line and as close to the upper left corner as possible. According to the ROC curve, first, compared to the Linear Kernel SVM, both models are much more effective on the Cyber Insurance dataset – this time the accuracy was a good measurement. Without any cost decisions the more expensive polynomial should be chosen here as the performance is a bit better than the RBF. But if the dataset is getting bigger, it should be focused on the RBF.

8.3.10 K-Nearest Neighbors

In the following, we will use the K-Nearest Neighbors (KNN) algorithm. The KNN algorithm is certainly one of the simplest and most efficient algorithms in ML (Altman, 1992). As with many non-parametric algorithms, the instances are represented here as points in multidimensional space. An instance is defined by its attributes. Each attribute represents an axis in multidimensional space, the number of occurrences of the attributes is merged into a point vector. With the KNN method, as the name already suggests, the decision is made based on the closest data to the point to be reassigned (Samworth, 2012).

As we performed the KNN on our Cyber Insurance dataset, we achieved an accuracy of 85% on the training data. Again, we want to evaluate this performance in a better way. Therefore, we want to look again at the ROC curve but this time also on the confusion matrix (Fawcett, 2006). With this approach, it is counted how many times a class is classified as a claim and how often not. To perform this task on the dataset, we are choosing cross-validation predicting function in Scikit-Learn. This function performs the validation and puts out the prediction on each training set fold. It is used to track the overfitting problem as described before. This is done by using the cross-validation parameter k in the library. We achieved the best result with K = 4. The performance obtained in this case is as follows:

KNN Confusion Matrix ([[239, 141],
  [76, 494]])

Each row in the confusion matrix is a current class, and each column represents a predicted class. The first row of the matrix describes 239 not claims (true negatives), correctly classified, but 141 were wrongly classified as claims (false positives). The second row considers (positive class) 76 cases, which were wrongly classified as non-claims (false negatives). Finally, 494 were correctly classified as claims (true positives). A perfect classifier would have only true positives and true negatives as an output.

At the ROC curve (Figure 8.4d), we can see that the performance is close to the polynomial SVM, but instead of the high computational cost we have a cheaper algorithm which can achieve this score.

8.3.11 Random Forest

Next, we will have a look at the Random Forest. A Random Forest is a classification process that consists of several uncorrelated decision trees. All decision trees have grown under a certain type of randomization during the learning process (Ho, 1995). For a classification, each tree in that forest may decide, and the class with the most votes decides the final classification. A single decision tree brings the problem of high variance with it. This means that if a tree is trained on one half of the training data and another tree on the other half, they can look very different. In general, this can be described in ML as overfitting (Ho, 1998). Among other things, this has a negative effect on the generality of the prediction of a decision tree. Random Forest, in contrast, uses feature bagging (Breimann et al., 2001) so that each forest considers a randomly selected subset of the available data. The results of each individual forest are then averaged, resulting in a flat output that allows deviations to be minimized. Bagging is used for a more stable prediction result. Bagging means the use of an ensemble of parallel estimators, where each of these estimators overfits the data and averages the results. In this case, trees are trained on samples of the training data generated by bootstraping. These trees are combined using a mean value. So, Random Forest relies on aggregating the result of an ensemble of simple estimators (Géron, 2017). The resulting sum is greater than its parts, as the sum is the majority voting from a lot of estimators that can end up being better than the vote of an estimator alone.

To apply the algorithm to the existing datasets, Scikit-Learn and the Random Forest Classifier class were used. The structure of Random Forest allows various adjustable parameters which are reflected in the tree depth, the leaves of the trees, and the branches and splits (Géron, 2017). These parameters are valuable when it comes to adjusting the model for the best possible accuracy. We first looked at four parameters individually to get a general overview of how they affect accuracy. From our model approach, the following parameters of adjustment realizations can be obtained. First, the distribution of the min_samples_split should remain at the lowest allowable value, which is 2. Similarly, the reduction of both the minimum_impurity_decrease and the minimum_weight_fraction of the data shows no benefit from the increase, so both are set to 0. Both the maximum_leaf_nodes and the maximum_depth indicate that they should be set relatively high to capture the descriptive performance in the dataset. Finally, the Min_Sample_Leaf shows a high variance for already small changes in the parameter value. A low value close to the default value of 1 is optimal. In addition, large values of maximum_depth lead to an overfitting of the training dataset, so we take care to avoid this high variance situation. One last parameter that has a big influence on the Random Forest result is the maximum_features (Bernard et al., 2009). In all our adjustments, increasing the number of trees leads to a higher accuracy only until a certain point (n_estimators = 1,000). As we took care to not overfit our model, this number for Random Forest was set of well-fit trees. In addition, the training time increases rapidly, thus the number of trees (n_estimators) is not so much a parameter, as a trade-off between training time and accuracy adjustments. As a result of our adjustments in our model, an accuracy of 100% was achieved on the training set. We will consider again the ROC and the confusion matrix. Comparing with the KNN algorithm, we achieved a hugely better result.

Random Forest Classifier Confusion Matrix ([[335, 96],
    [59, 546]])

The first row of the matrix describes 335 not claims (true negatives) which is an almost 100 cases better than the KNN did correctly, and we have less (96) wrongly classified as claims (false positives) classes than we reached before.

Also, the second row (positive class) reduces to 59 cases that were wrongly classified as non-claims (false negatives). Finally, also a raise of 48 in contrast to the KNN, and here are now 546 sets that were correctly classified as claims (true positives).

There are few parameters left to adjust the ML algorithm. Boosting for instance is a process that provides an efficient decision rule for a classification problem by combining several simple rules. The result, however, that is, the accurate decision rule, is called a strong classifier. The idea of using boosting methods for classification problems is relatively new (Schapire, 1990). AdaBoost has delivered amazingly good results for all classification problems. Therefore, we want to test this method also on our Cyber Insurance dataset. The AdaBoost classifier can be build up on a Decision Tree Classifier in Scikit-Learn and is performed on sequential trainings. Although, the results of boosting are very interesting, we have made the experience that the computational resources are very big, and the results which were made (Figure 8.4e–8.4g) show that the ROC for the Random Forest Classifier itself were better.

Even the confusion matrix results make this conclusion – although it is very close to the Gradient Boosting results, as only the wrongly classified and true positives differ.

Adaboost Confusion Matrix ([[316, 115],
   [90, 515]])
Gradient Boosting Confusion Matrix ([[335, 96],
   [85, 520]])

To further understand how to interpret the performance of the random forest algorithm, it is applied based on unused customer datasets. Here, based on the case from the customer data records, we generate the prediction of a future claim: Insurance Claim Probability array [0.109, 0.891] and Insurance Claim Prediction array [1]. That means that the dataset has a 11% chance of being class 0 and 89% chance of being class 1.

Many model forms describe the underlying impact of features relative to each other. In Scikit-Learn, Decision Tree models and ensembles of trees such as Random Forest provide a feature importance attribute when fitted. This utilizes this attribute to rank and plot relative importance. Our research results show (Figure 8.4h) the use of forests of trees to evaluate the importance of features on an artificial classification task. The red bars are the feature importance of the forest, along with their inter-tree's variability. The plot suggests that the most important features is CC/PII data, where all the other features are equally important, Other IT insurance is not.

8.4 Model Selection

This work has analyzed several ML approaches to assess companies' cyber risk insurability.

As demonstrated along the chapter, the best performance was achieved with the classification algorithm and with the Random Forest classifier. In order to evaluate and compare the appropriate choice of the training set as well as the test set, we will make a ranking based on the obtained results, and with this we can create an even better algorithm for our Cyber Insurance dataset. This can be done by aggregating the predictions of each classifier and predict the class by means of the most votes. With Scikit-Learn, a majority or also hard voting can be performed to achieve this result. Even if each classifier would be a weak learner by means of aggregation, it can be a strong learning achieved. Even a better result (Table 8.4) was achieved by means of soft voting. After achieving 100% at the training set, the Random Forest as well as the Voting Classifier achieve 87 and 88%, respectively, on the test dataset.

Our learning methods Random Forest and Gradient Boosting showed similar results, with Random Forest having an advantage. Both are ensemble methods that train many models and obtain results for each one, but they follow different approaches to aggregating

Table 8.4   Results after Performing Soft Voting

Gradient Boosting Classifier	0.861
Random Forest Classifier	0.873
AdaBoost Classifier	0.826
Voting Classifier	0.876

their results. Random Forest uses bootstrap aggregation (bagging), which consists of simply selecting a subset. Gradient Boosting goes one step further by boosting certain data points so that they have a greater effect on the resulting model. Whenever a data point in a Gradient Boosting is misclassified, subsequent runs will weight that point higher so that it is highlighted. This sequential learning gives Gradient Boosting an advantage over Random Forest. For our Cyber Insurance dataset entry forecast, however, the Random Forrest is somewhat better and with a use of less computer resources.

8.5 Conclusion

Today's Cyber Insurance underwriting is human-based processing of data. In technical underwriting, this approach is still important as technical underwriting means assessing current risks and established countermeasures at each company, and technical underwriting needs interaction with key stakeholders. On the other hand, economic underwriting is based on few static values so far, even though data breaches and Cyber Incidents are steadily increasing. This chapter surveys various ML algorithms and introduces most of the popular ML algorithms in the context of growing Cyber Insurance demand. The results of the analysis on the customer dataset are encouraging in general.

It can be noted that in the context of the available Cyber Insurance data, no meaningful results were achieved with regression algorithms. We experienced the same with Logistic Regression and Linear SVM Classifier. Thus, these algorithms are not considered any further (Table 8.5).

With Gaussian RBF SVM, Polynomial SVM, KNN algorithms, we achieve meaningful results, and therefore, more research will be considered. Same approach will be used on the best performing

Table 8.5 ML Algorithms – No Further Consideration

Linear Regression
Lasso Regression
Ridge Regression
Logistic Regression
Linear Kernel SVM Classifier

Table 8.6   ML Algorithms – For Further Consideration

Random Forest Classifier
Gradient Boosting Classifier
AdaBoost Classifier
Gaussian RBF SVM
Polynomial SVM
K-Nearest Neighbors

algorithms based on our research: the Random Forest Classifier, Gradient Boosting Classifier, AdaBoost Classifier (Table 8.6).

Further research will concentrate on feature engineering on these algorithms and possible approaches with Machine Learning Platform (MLP) at Deep Neural Networks as well.

References

Alpaydin, E. (2010). *Introduction to machine learning*, 2nd. ed. Cambridge: The MIT Press.

Altman, N. (1992). An introduction to kernel and nearest-neighbor non-parametric regression. *The American Statistician*, *46(3)*, pp. 175–185. Doi:10.2307/2685209.

Bartolini, D.N., Benavente-Peces, C., Ahrens, A. (2017). *Risk assessment and verification of insurability*. Proceedings of the 7th International Joint Conference on Pervasive and Embedded Computing and Communication Systems. (PECCS 2017). Madrid: July 24-26, pp. 105–108.

Bartolini, D.N., Zascerinska, J., Benavente-Peces, CJ., Ahrens, A. (2018). Instrument design for cyber risk assessment in insurability verification. *Informatics, Control, Measurement in Economy and Environment Protection*, *3*, pp. 7–10. Doi.org/10.5604/01.3001.0012.5274.

Bernard, S., Heutte, L., Adam, S. (2009). *Influence of Hyperparameters on Random Forest Accuracy*. International Workshop on Multiple Classifier Systems (MCS). Reykjavik, Iceland: June, pp.171–180. https://hal.archives-ouvertes.fr/hal-00436358/document.

Bishop, C.M. (2006). *Pattern recognition and machine learning (information science and statistics)*. Berlin, Heideberg: Springer-Verlag.

Boyd, S., Vandenberghe, L. (2004). *Convex optimization*. USA: Cambridge University Press.

Breiman, L. (2001). Random forests. *Machine Learning*, *45*, pp. 5–32. Doi. org/10.1023/A:1010933404324.

Breiman, L., Friedman, J. (1997). Predicting multivariate responses in multiple linear regression. *Journal of the Royal Statistical Society. Series B (Methodological)*, *59(1)*, pp. 3–54. Retrieved from: http://www.jstor.org/stable/2345915. (Access: 19.01.2020).

Bühlmann, P., van de Geer, S. (2011). *Statistics for high-dimensional data.* Berlin, Heideberg: Springer.

Burnham, K., Anderson, D.R. (2002). *Model selection and multimodel inference: A practical information-theoretic approach.* New York, NY: Springer-Verlag Inc. Doi.org/10.1007/B97636.

Chang, Y.W., Hsieh, C.J., Chang, K.W. (2010). Training and testing low-degree polynomial data mappings via linear SVM. *Journal of Machine Learning Research, 11*, pp. 1471–1490.

Cortes, C., Vapnik, V. (1995). Support-vector networks. *Machine Learning, 20*, pp. 273–297. Dx.doi.org/10.1007/BF00994018.

Domingos, P. (2012). A few useful things to know about machine learning. *Communications of the ACM, 55*, pp. 78–87. Doi: 10.1145/2347736. 2347755.

Fawcett, T. (2006). An Introduction to ROC analysis. *Pattern Recognition Letters, 27*, pp. 861–874. Doi: 10.1016/j.patrec.2005.10.010.

General Data Protection Regulation. (2016). Final Version. Retrieved from: http://ec.europa.eu/justice/data-protection/reform/files/regulation_oj_en.pdf. (Access: 28.11.2019).

Géron, A. (2017). *Hands-on machine learning with Scikit-Learn and Tensor Flow: Concepts, tools, and techniques to build intelligent systems.* Sebastopol, CA: O'Reilly Media.

Goldberg, Y., Elhadad, M. (2008). *SplitSVM: Fast, space-efficient, non-heuristic, polynomial kernel computation for NLP applications.* Proceedings of the 46st Annual Meeting of the Association of Computational Linguistics (ACL), pp. 237–240.

Harrell, F.E. (2001). *Regression modeling strategies: With applications to linear models, logistic regression, and survival analysis.* New York, NY: Springer.

Helmbold, D., Sloan, R., Warmuth, M.K. (1990) Learning nested differences of intersection-closed concept classes. *Machine Learning 5*, pp. 165–196. Doi:10.1007/BF00116036.

Ho, T.K. (1995). *Random decision forest.* Proceedings of the 3rd International Conference on Document Analysis and Recognition. Montreal: August, pp. 278–282.

Ho, T.K. (1998). The random subspace method for constructing decision forests. *IEEE Trans. Pattern Anal. Mach. Intell., 20*, pp. 832–844.

Muller, K.R. (2012). Active learning with model selection. In: M., Sugiyama, M. Kawanabe (eds.), *Machine learning in non-stationary environments: Introduction to covariate shift adaptation.* Cambridge: The MIT Press, pp. 215–224.

Muller, K.R. (2017). In *caseFrom measurement to machine learning: Towards analysing cognition*, 5th International Winter Conference on Brain-Computer Interface, IEEE, Book Series: International Winter Workshop on Brain-Computer Interface. Sabuk, South Korea, pp. 53–54.

PCI Security Standards Council. (2018). Payment Card Industry (PCI) Data Security Standard Requirements and Security Assessment Procedures Version 3.2.1.

Raschka, S., Mirjalili, V. (2019). *Python machine learning: Machine learning and deep learning with Python, Scikit-Learn, and Tensorflow 2*, 3rd ed. Birmingham: Packt.

Rud, O. (2009). *Business intelligence success factors: Tools for aligning your business in the global economy.* Hoboken, Ney Jersey: John Wiley & Sons Inc.

Samworth, R.J. (2012). Optimal weighted nearest neighbour classifiers. *The Annals of Statistics, 40(5)*, pp. 2733–2763. Doi: 10.1214/12-AOS1049.

Santosa, F., Symes, W.W. (1989). An analysis of least-squares velocity inversion. *Geophysical Monograph Series.* Tulsa: Society of Exploration Geophysicists.

Schapire, R.E. (1990). The strength of weak learnability. *Machine Learning, 5(2)*, pp. 197–227.

Scikit-Learn. (2019). Documentation. 2019.

Tibshirani, R. (1996). Regression shrinkage and selection via the lasso. *Journal of the Royal Statistical Society (Series B), 58*, pp. 267–288.

Tikhonov, A.N. (1963). Solution of incorrectly formulated problems and the regularization method. *Soviet Mathematics Doklady, 4*, pp. 1035–1038.

Yan, X. (2009). *Linear regression analysis: Theory and computing.* Singapore: World Scientific Publishing Company Pte. Ltd.

9

APPLIED DATA ANALYTICS

CÉSAR BENAVENTE-PECES,
DAVID NICOLAS BARTOLINI,
GALYNA TABUNSHCHYK, AND
NATALIA MYRONOVA

Contents

9.1 Introduction

Decision-making algorithms are playing the significant role in the implementation of the digitalization strategies in the different fields particularly in business analytics. Big Data analytics is an ecosystem of technologies that allows the collection, storage, and exploitation of large volumes of data that are generated at different speeds and have different varieties of information, both structured and unstructured (blogs, social networks, videos, images, etc.).

This setup allows to have a very flexible platform that operates as a unified repository of information that reduces costs and serves as the basis to give business solutions to a wide range of requirements (analysis, event correlation, exploitation, transformation, business intelligence [BI], and client 360) that allows to exploit Tb of information with thousands of operations per second and in real time.

Data scientists are the advanced analytics experts who give value to data. Through their work, companies can face new challenges, predict future situations, bet on the best alternatives, provide better services to customers, and maximize profits.

More and more Big Data projects are being developed by the three "Vs" (Volume, Variety, and Velocity), but do we know how the new General Data Protection Regulation (GDPR) impacts these systems?

Data analytics techniques extract relevant information of data and try to obtain any feature which would help for different purposes, for example, to model the data by extracting statistical characteristics. Once the behavior of a parameter is modelled, we can predict its value under a given situation.

The exploitation of large amounts of data, including personal data, using a set of technologies, systems, and algorithms, is booming, as it allows, in the face of an enormous volume of data, to extract valuable information for studies: retrospective, prospective, commercial projections, establishment of profiles, and usage patterns (both for statistical and scientific and commercial purposes), etc. The results of these analysis can have a direct impact on people, which is why they are increasingly becoming a matter of concern, and regulation is necessary to safeguard the privacy of people in Big Data models.

9.2 Big Data

Big Data is an emerging trend, which is attracting the attention of scientists, industry, organizations, governments, and individuals. The motivations will be different, but the basis is the same: capability to achieve and store heterogeneous data to be processed in different ways to extract meaningful information.

Big Data refers to datasets that are not only big but also high in variety and velocity, which makes them difficult to handle using traditional tools and techniques (Elgendy and Elragal, 2014).

Since the beginning of the digital society, the information society, the availability of data, either captured in real time or stored in large databases, increases. Researchers both in social science and scientific science, and decision makers in general, are eager to manage amounts of data in order to refine or achieve more accurate results (e.g., medical diagnosis, people behavior, artificial intelligence [AI], system modelling, etc.).

The term Big Data regards more than just large amounts, but their heterogeneous nature, the availability of data coming from different sources, captured at different rates or speeds, are difficult to manage (Angierski and Kuehn, 2013). In consequence, innovative techniques must be provided in order to achieve a better performance. Current research trends point to the use of novel methods and techniques to manage such huge amount of data, which is in continuous and fast growth due to endless data generation, which must be extracted from raw data, preprocessed, managed and stored in databases, and finally processed to make decisions, in the framework of their final usage (Srinivasa and Mehta, 2014).

Those novel techniques should provide decision makers with valuable tools to extract the relevant information which seems to be hidden to traditional approaches, especially in those cases where the data has a high volatility, and the sophisticated algorithms must be fast and agile. Big Data analytics can be the appropriate toolkit aimed at providing the additional value to Big Data (Pyne et al., 2016).

As the Big Data problem is understood in greater depth, the definition of what we understand by Big Data becomes more precise, and greater the need for more appropriate tools for data analysis. However, the nuances of the Big Data definition are conditioned by the final application, the characteristics and properties of the data, and their nature and origin, so there will not be a standard definition applied in all cases, but they will have nuances depending on the problem to solve. We can take as an example the definition that authors propose regarding their work on quality in Big Data (Emmanuel and Stanier, 2016).

The three "Vs" of Big Data reflect the challenge that big companies face when it comes to giving data a value to make better decisions, improve operations, and reduce risks. Therefore, it is necessary to be able to navigate easily to obtain information both within the company's systems and the data that arrives from outside.

If we analyze Big Data projects, they generally follow the following phases:

- Data collection (which may involve buying and selling information).
- The verification and validation of the data.
- Storage (both initial and resulting data).
- The analysis and exploitation of the results.

There are several final applications where Big Data-based techniques are being applied with different purposes. Among them, we can highlight the following:

- Understanding and segmenting customers: Marketing and sales are perhaps the areas of greatest application of Big Data today. The data is used to better understand customers, their behaviors, and preferences. Companies are willing to expand traditional data centers with those of social networks, navigation logs, text analysis, and sensor data to get a complete picture of their client. The main objective in most cases is to create predictive models.
- Understanding and optimizing business processes: Big Data is increasingly being used to optimize business processes in companies. In the retail sector, businesses are optimizing their stock based on predictions generated thanks to social network data, web search trends, and weather forecasts. A process that is being transformed particularly thanks to Big Data is that of the supply chain and the optimization of delivery routes.

- Quantification and optimization of personal performance: Big Data is not only for companies, public institutions, or large organizations. We all can benefit from the data generated from wearable devices such as smart watches or bracelets.
- Improving public health: Another area of collective mass data use is the coding of genetic material. The more the users are involved, the more the benefits are obtained, either to know more about our ancestors, whose diet or food is most suitable for our genotype, or to discover how or why certain genes that can lead to chronic diseases are activated. The processing capacity of Big Data analysis platforms allows us to decode entire chains of DNA in a matter of minutes and will allow us to find new treatments and better understand diseases, their triggers, and propagation patterns.
- Improving sports performance: Most elite athletes are already adopting high-volume data analysis techniques. In tennis, it has been a long time of using the SlamTracker tool (based on IBM SPSS predictive analysis technology) in the most prestigious tournaments in the world (Wimbledon, Roland Garros, and Australian Open).
- Improving science and research: Scientific research is being transformed by the new possibilities offered by Big Data.
- Optimizing the performance of machines and devices: Big Data analysis is helping machines and devices to be more intelligent and autonomous.
- Improving security and law enforcement: Big Data analysis is being used intensively to improve security and law enforcement. The news leaked via Wikileaks revealed that the National Security Agency (NSA) has been spying on all the communications of all citizens. The objective is the protection against terrorist attacks.
- Improving and optimizing cities: Big Data is also being used to improve aspects of our cities and countries. The technology allows to optimize traffic flows based on data that arrives in real time from traffic, social networks, and weather.
- Financial trading: The last area of examples of use of Big Data that we are going to review, although not of smaller volume

or importance, is that of the application of Big Data in capital markets. The activities related to High-Frequency Trading (HFT) is where there is the greatest use of Big Data.

In our case, we are going to apply the data analysis techniques to determine the cyber risk that a certain company has against possible external attacks on its computer systems and databases (Bartolini et al., 2017a). Until now, this evaluation procedure was carried out through a questionnaire and required the consumption of human resources and time. The objective is to systematize this evaluation by reducing the impact of the subjective analysis on the person in charge of the evaluation in some critical factors, which can lead to inaccuracies in the evaluation result.

9.3 Data Analytics Techniques

In this section, a brief introduction to data analytics techniques is drawn to make some remarks. First, a definition of the term data analytics is needed to understand the problem to be faced. Data analytics is defined as the process for cleaning, transforming, and modeling collected data to point out relevant information for decision-making.

There are several types of data analysis techniques that exist based on business and technology. The major types of data analysis are as follows:

- Text analysis.
- Statistical analysis.
- Diagnostic analysis.
- Predictive analysis.
- Prescriptive analysis.

These techniques can be applied for different purposes, and depending on the problem to be solved and the significance of the collected datasets, the appropriate technique must be applied.

9.4 Cyber Risk Assessments

In this section, the powerful Big Data analytics tool will be applied to support decision makers in cyber insurance companies (Bartolini et al., 2017b).

Cyber risks primarily affect digital information security, but also any source of information independently of its nature. Cyber risk can jeopardize the availability, integrity, and confidentiality of sensitive data, processes, and information when it is realized.

The approach chosen in the work described in this chapter explores the features of factors related to cyber risk and cyber security, and tries to identify which factors more significantly impact the insurers' economic risk assessment (Bartolini et al., 2018a). The selection criteria adopted in our approach point out the following set of features as the most appropriate:

- The *Turnover*, as per definition, means "the aggregate value of the realization of amount made from the sale, supply, or distribution of goods or on account of services rendered, or both, by the company during a financial year." Basically, it concerns the company benefits. Usually, big companies require large IT infrastructures and the Turnover is higher than in small ones. In addition, a large and well-known company is more exposed to a cyber-attack than a small one.
- *Other IT insurances* regards companies which contract additional insurances. This factor, for an economic as well as a risk-based approach, is relevant because given the company has more IT insurances besides the cyber insurance and if this additional risk transfer has a positive correlation.
- *Credit card/cardholder and personal identifying information (CC/PII)* data. Hosting this personal information is a risk for the company given in the case of successful cyber-attack these data can be stolen, the insurance company should attend the claims, and the company reputation will drop.
- Data breaches have dramatic outcomes in which personal data as well as cardholder data are stolen by criminals. Claims payments can arise when the company is forced to pay fines in the legal context (e.g., GDPR) or in the regulatory context (e.g., Payment Card Industry Data Security Standard [PCI DSS]).
- The result of the technical cyber risk assessment is the *Rating*. As described in previous related work (Bartolini et al., 2018b), a company can be technically insured if the result of the cyber risk assessment (technical risk assessment) reaches

the minimum Rating score 2.00. Therefore, this criterion is the one used to decide whether to proceed with the insurance contract or not. The Rating depends on the other factors mentioned in this work.

- *Critical infrastructures (KRITIS)* are organizational and physical structures and facilities of such vital importance to a nation's society and economy that their failure or degradation would result in sustained supply shortages, significant disruption of public safety and security, or other dramatic consequences. The customer is one of the critical infrastructures. As critical infrastructures are a high target for criminals, these companies need to have a high maturity level.

- *Investments in IT/Cyber Programs* is another economic factor to be considered in the correlation analysis. In general, the investment in IT makes the whole infrastructure more robust and protected against cyber-attacks, and the cyber risk drops noticeably.

- In the case a cyber-attack succeeds, a damage finally is produced. In consequence, the insurance company must compensate the damages. The factor called cyber *Insurance claim* concerns the expenses when the damage has occurred at the company. It is a very important aspect to consider in the approach.

9.4.1 *Analysis of Cyber Security-Related Data*

The term "cyber risk" refers to a multitude of different sources of risk affecting the information and technology assets of a firm. Cyber risk can be categorized according to different criteria. A detailed categorization is provided at Biener et al. (2015).

The data used to assess whether a company can be insured in relation to cyber security has been presented previously. It is about observing the risk of suffering a cyber-attack and the damage and economic cost that would impact the insurance company, given the compensation that it should provide to those affected.

For this, the interdependencies between the different parameters that have already been identified as relevant when assessing the possibility of insuring a company against possible cyber-attacks, that is, cyber risk, should be analyzed.

In the first phase, the parameter data will be carried out individually in order to obtain the most relevant characteristics. In the second phase, the dependencies between the data will be analyzed in order to identify which ones have the greatest weight in the decision-making process and in the establishment of an adequate model.

Probability distribution functions are used as part of a set of analytical tools. The beginning of its employment dates to the 19th century. Figures 9.1a÷9.1g show the probability distribution functions of the parameters used to analyze and evaluate the contract of cyber insurance. The analysis of the probability distribution functions can allow us to infer which would be the most appropriate analysis regarding the regression model to be applied. In some cases, a logistic regression should be applied, given the characteristics of some of the variables. In other cases, a deeper analysis will have to be done to determine whether it is convenient to use the linear regression of one or several variables, or another type.

Figure 9.1d shows the probability distribution function of the Rating, and most companies (more than 80%) obtain a *Rating* of 3. On the other hand, approximately in the sixth part, 14% of companies obtain a *Rating* of 2, which implies a high risk of being sensitive to cyber-attacks, cyber risk.

9.4.2 Linear Regression: Identifying Linear Dependencies

The least squares method consists in calculating the sum of the squared distances between the real points and the points defined by the estimated line from the variables introduced in the model so that the best estimate will be the one that minimizes these distances. In order to decide which model is best suited to the data available in the linear regression model, the partial results obtained in each of the constructed regression models are compared. If we use any of the techniques of selection of previously exposed variables, this coefficient will be calculated each time a variable is eliminated or introduced, since when performing this process, new regression models will be estimated. In all cases, the statistical package performs the operation

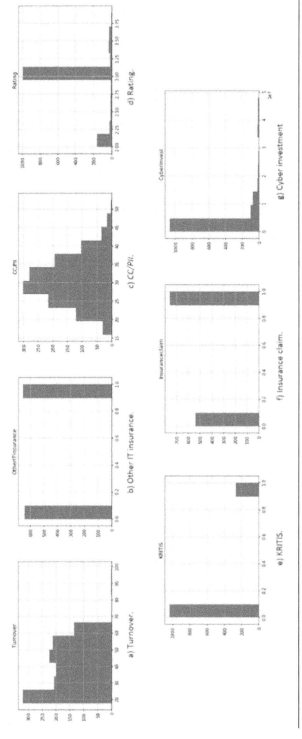

Figure 9.1 Probability distribution function for the different parameters.

automatically, except if we use the technique of forcing all variables to enter, in which case we will be estimating all possible models manually to subsequently make the selection.

For the application of a linear regression model to be appropriate, it must be satisfied that the response values (*y*) are independent of each other and the relationship between the variables is linear, as follows:

$$y = \beta_1 \cdot x_1 + \varepsilon \qquad (9.1)$$

An example of a linear dependency is Figure 9.2a, which depicts the relation (dependency) between the *Turnover* and the *Cyber Invest*. The linear dependency is given in steps, so the model becomes a bit more complex than just a line.

Figure 9.2b shows the relationship between Turnover and CC/PII. In this case, a simple linear relationship between the two variables is not observed, so we must look for other models that are somewhat more complex.

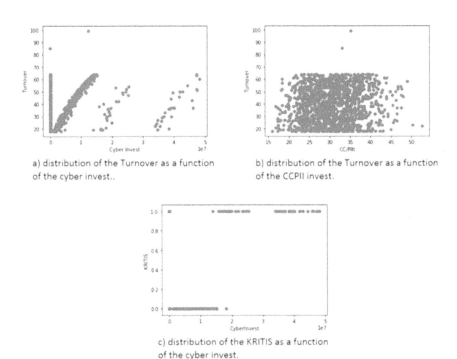

a) distribution of the Turnover as a function of the cyber invest..

b) distribution of the Turnover as a function of the CCPII invest.

c) distribution of the KRITIS as a function of the cyber invest.

Figure 9.2   Dependencies among the most relevant parameters.

9.4.3 Logistic Regression: When Managing Logical Parameters

The identification of the best logistic regression model is done by comparing models using the quotient and likelihood, which indicates from the sample data that one model is more likely to go against the other. The difference of the likelihood ratios between the two models is distributed according to the Chi-square law with the degrees of freedom corresponding to the difference in the number of variables between both the models. If it cannot be demonstrated from this coefficient that one model is better than the other, then the simplest will be considered as the most appropriate. The linear regression model results in a quantitative variable. If the output variable is qualitative, it cannot be applied directly.

For example, a qualitative variable, called "Other IT Insurance," which indicates whether other additional insurance has been contracted: "YES" or "NO." Then, two groups are defined:

0 = NO. They have not contracted additional insurance.

1 = YES. They have hired an additional insurance.

In this case, linear regression cannot be applied to solve the problem. We cannot draw a cloud of points as in the case of linear regression. To solve the problem, we must transform the output variable with the logistics operator.

This mathematical operator tries to convert the group 0 or 1 for a probability that they have contracted additional insurance or not. In this way, we transform the qualitative variable into the number, which is a probability. Afterward, we can use the same structure as in the linear regression. We are simply transforming the qualitative response variable into a quantitative one.

We applied the logistic regression to our variable called "Other IT Insurance," and we obtained the following results, as depicted in Figure 9.3a and Figure 9.3b. These figures show the main features of the logistic regression for *Other IT Insurance*. Among those relevant features, we remark the precision and recall for the cases of micro average, macro average, and weighted average. *Precision* is a measure of the accuracy provided that a class label has been predicted. It is defined by *precision* = $TP/(TP + FP)$, where TP states for true positive, and FP states for false positive. Recall is the true positive rate. It is defined as: *Recall* = $TP/(TP + FN)$, where FN states for false negative.

	precision	recall	f1-score	support
0	0.00	0.00	0.00	133
1	0.49	1.00	0.66	127
micro avg	0.49	0.49	0.49	260
macro avg	0.24	0.50	0.33	260
weighted avg	0.24	0.49	0.32	260

a) Features of the logistic regression
for Other IT Insurance..

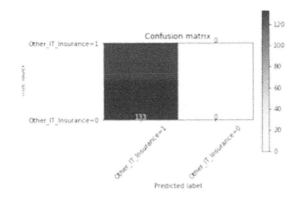

b) Confusion matrix obtained in the logistic
regression of Other IT Insurance..

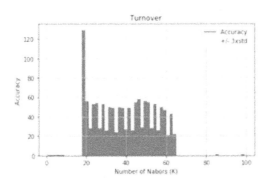

c) Accuracy of Turnover estimation vs. K.

Figure 9.3   Features of the logistic regression.

This parameter takes 1,0, so there are no false negative predictions. On the other hand, a considerable number of false positive values are produced, revealing that the prediction accuracy is low.

In order to interpret the result of the logistic regression model, we must resort to the concept of "odds," one of the measures available to quantify the risk. In this way, the "odds" is defined as the quotient of the probability of presenting a characteristic and the probability of not presenting it, that is, the number of cases showing the characteristic to the number of cases which don't ratio.

The performance of a given model is explained through evaluation metrics. At the most basic level, the assessment of a certain model can compare the actual values versus the predicted values, and the difference will serve to determine the accuracy of the regression model. Hence, evaluation metrics play a relevant role in the process of model development. The evaluation metrics make an insight pointing out how the accuracy can be improved.

9.4.4 K-Nearest Neighbors Classifier

K-Nearest Neighbors is an algorithm for supervised learning, where the data is "trained" with data points corresponding to their classification. Once a point is to be predicted, it considers the "K" nearest points to it to determine its classification. The typical dataset of this type of algorithm is made up of several descriptive attributes and a single objective attribute (also called class).

In our problem, we are going to show how it is applied on the *Turnover*. Its probability distribution function was depicted in Figure 9.1a. The goal is to build a classifier to be able to predict the class of unknown cases. To do this, we select a specific type of classifier, which is called K-Nearest Neighbors. From the set of available data, we arrange them in the following way:

- Train set: 1,036 couples of values, with K = 6.
- Test set: 260 couples of values, with K = 6.
- Train set accuracy: 0.28667953667953666.
- Test set accuracy: 0.05384615384615385.

The result of the algorithm for classification draws that the best accuracy is 0.07307692307692308, which is obtained with K = 2.

9.4.5 Decision Tree

Decision Trees are a non-parametric supervised learning method used for classification and regression. The objective is to create a model that predicts the value of an objective variable by learning simple decision rules inferred from the characteristics of the data.

For example, decision trees learning from the data can approximate a sinusoidal curve with a set of *if-then-else* decision rules. The deeper the tree is, the more complex the decision rules will be and the more appropriate the model will be.

The decision trees have a first node called root (root), and then the other input attributes are broken down into two branches (they could be more, but we will not get into that now) posing a condition that may be true or false. Each node is forked in two, and they are subdivided again until they reach the leaves that are the final nodes and that are equivalent to answers to the solution: *Yes/No, Buy/Sell*, or whatever we are classifying.

Some of the advantages of decision trees are as follows:

- Easy to understand and interpret. Trees can be visualized.
- They require little data preparation. Other techniques often require data normalization, the creation of dummy variables, and the elimination of blank values. Note, however, that this module does not support the missing values.
- The cost of using the tree (i.e., predicting data) is logarithmic in the number of data points used to train the tree.
- Able to handle numerical and categorical data. Other techniques are usually specialized in the analysis of datasets that only have one type of variable.
- Able to handle multiple exit problems.
- Use a white box model. If a given situation is observable in a model, the explanation of the condition is easily explained by Boolean logic. On the contrary, in a black box model (e.g., in an artificial neural network), the results may be more difficult to interpret.
- Possibility of validating a model through statistical tests. This allows to account for the reliability of the model.
- It works well even if your assumptions are somewhat violated by the true model from which the data was generated.

Disadvantages of decision trees include the following:

- Parameters in the decision tree can create too complex trees that do not generalize the data well. This is called over-equipment. Mechanisms such as pruning (not currently supported), setting the minimum number of samples required in a leaf knot, or setting the maximum depth of the tree are necessary to avoid this problem.
- Decision trees can be unstable because small variations in the data can result in the generation of a completely different tree. This problem is mitigated by using decision trees within a set.
- The problem of learning an optimal decision tree is known to be nondeterministic polynomial (NP)-complete under various aspects of optimization and even for simple concepts. Consequently, the practical learning algorithms of the decision tree are based on heuristic algorithms such as the greedy algorithm, in which optimal decisions are made at the local level at each node. Such algorithms cannot guarantee that they return the globally optimal decision tree. This can be mitigated by training multiple trees in a group of students, where characteristics and samples are randomly sampled with replacement.
- There are concepts that are difficult to learn because decision trees do not express them easily, such as OR exclusive (XOR), parity, or multiplexer problems.
- Decision tree participants create biased trees if some classes dominate. Therefore, it is recommended to balance the dataset before adjusting it to the decision tree.

In this case, we focus our attention on the assessment result, the *Rating*, based on the input parameters, *Turnover*, which gives an idea about how is a company exposed to a cyber-attack, *Other IT insurances* that the company has contracted, *CC/PII* data hosted by the company, the *Cyber Investment* which the company has spent to improve its information and communications technology (ICT) infrastructures and security to reduce cyber risk, KRITIS, the *Insurance claim* the company has faced due to successful cyber-attacks. The Train set is composed of 907 inputs-target sets, while the Test set is composed of 389 inputs-target sets.

In the approach shown in this work, we used the given Rating parameter as a goal. This finally leads to the decision contract/do-not-contract based on the achieved Rating. So, in future investigations and developments, we will first categorize and map the Rating score into YES/NO decision, which is the first step toward the process automation.

To optimize the process, further analysis of the different parameters used to build the decision tree is needed to find out features that lead to better and optimal solutions.

Figure 9.4 shows the resulting decision tree. Some remarks must be drawn to fully understand the given result. When analyzing the problem and implementing a solution, we faced two possibilities: either using a Decision Tree Classifier or a Decision Tree Regressor. The first approach requires the target to be clearly organized in categories or, for example, binary decisions: YES/NO. Given the intention of this work is using the raw data provided by companies, that idea was left for further investigation, and we use the raw Rating data. So, we focus on the second approach, that is, using the Decision Tree Regressor to avoid preprocessing the data and get an open solution.

The decision involves some advantages/drawbacks, as follows:

- The main advantage is getting the decision in terms of a score in the range [0,4]. This criterion gives the opportunity to review the scores which are applied so far to make better and accurate decisions.
- The main drawback is that the score could not make the best decision.

9.4.6 Support Vector Machines

Support vector machines (SVMs) have their origin in the work on the theory of statistical learning and were introduced in the 90s by Vapnik and his collaborators (Boser et al., 1992; Cortes and Vapnik, 1995). Although SVMs were originally intended to solve binary classification problems, they are currently used to solve other types of problems (regression, grouping, and multiclassification). There are also diverse fields in which they have been used successfully, such as artificial vision, character recognition, categorization of hypertext text, protein

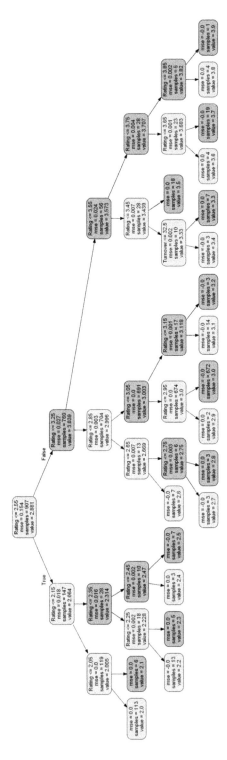

Figure 9.4   Decision tree resulting from training and test.

classification, natural language processing, and time series analysis. In fact, since its introduction, they have been earning a deserved recognition, thanks to their solid theoretical foundations.

SVM is a machine learning technique that finds the best possible separation between classes. With two dimensions, it is easy to understand what you are doing. Normally, machine learning problems have many dimensions. So, instead of finding the optimal line, the SVM finds the hyperplane that maximizes the margin of separation between classes.

The dataset used in this investigation consists of sample records concerning several hundred cyber risk assessment reports, each of which contains the values of a set of features related to cyber risk. The fields in each record are the ones described above, that is, *Turnover, Other IT Insurance, CC/PII, Rating, KRITIS, Cyber Invest.*

In the data analytics applied to this dataset, first we will analyze how *Cyber Investment* and *CC/PII* impact on the Insurance claims registered by companies which were affected in some way.

Figure 9.5a shows the relation of the insurance claims due to damages produced by succeeding cyber-attacks based on the company investment on cyber security and the risk of holding credit cards and personal data which are usually a target of cyber crimes. As expected, the more the investment in cyber security, the lower the success probability.

Further, continuing with the analysis, Figure 9.5b shows the scores which the algorithm obtains after its analysis.

Finally, Figure 9.5c shows the distribution of the confusion matrix based on the values of the Cyber Investment of the company and the CC/PII. It is worthy to note that the similarity score is 0.5423076923076923, when comparing the estimated values versus the test dataset.

9.5 Implementation of the Data Analytics Methods for the Forecast

To predict season diseases, either statistical or structural models can be used (Hyndman and Athanasopoulos, 2018).

Statistical methods considered in this investigation include the following:

- Classical Poisson method.
- Dickson-Coles method.

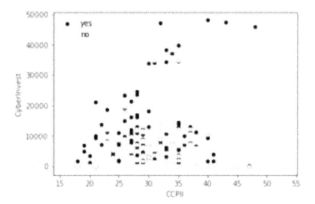

a) Distribution of the Insurance claim
based on CCPII and Cyberinvest.

	precision	recall	f1-score	support
0	0.45	0.21	29.00	114
1	0.57	0.80	0.66	146
accuracy			0.54	260
macro avg	0.51	0.51	0.48	260
weighted a	0.52	0.54	0.5	260

b) Evaluation scores.

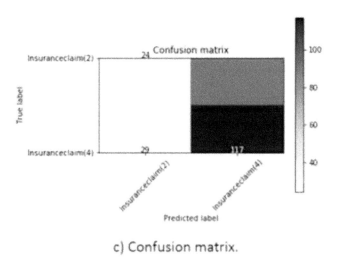

c) Confusion matrix.

Figure 9.5   Features of the decision tree.

- Least squares method.
- Autoregressive model of variable mean.
- Model of simple exponential smoothing.
- Holt exponential smoothing model.
- Holt-Winters exponential smoothing model.

On the other hand, from the existing structural methods the following were selected:

- Neural network with nonlinear autoregressive model.
- Multilayer perceptron with five hidden layers.
- Multilayer perceptron with automatic detection of the number of hidden layers.
- Machine of extreme training.

Besides the methods mentioned above, another classification could be applied:

- Regression models and methods.
- Autoregressive models and methods.
- Models and methods of exponential smoothing.
- Neural network models and methods.

According to the suggested classification in the Table 9.1, there are systemized strong and weak sides of above-mentioned approaches.

For the estimation of the accuracy of prediction methods, time series forecasting error rates will be used (Hyndman and Koehler, 2006).

Table 9.1 Comparison of the Methods and Models

MODEL AND METHOD	ADVANTAGES	DISADVANTAGES
Autoregressive models and methods	Simplicity, uniformity of analysis and design; numerous application examples	The complexity of model identification; impossibility of modelling nonlinearities; low adaptability
Models and methods of exponential smoothing	Simplicity, uniformity of analysis and design	Insufficient flexibility; narrow applicability of models
Neural network models and methods	Nonlinearity of models; scalability, high adaptability; uniformity of analysis and design; large set of examples	Lack of transparency; complexity of choice of architecture; stringent training sample requirements; the complexity of choosing a learning algorithm; resource-intensive learning process

The most common time series forecasting errors are as presented below:

MAPE – mean absolute percentage error:

$$MAPE = \frac{1}{N}\sum_{t=1}^{N}\frac{\left|X(t)-\hat{X}(t)\right|}{X(t)}\cdot 100\% \qquad (9.2)$$

MAE – mean absolute error:

$$MAE = \frac{1}{N}\sum_{t=1}^{N}\left|X(t)-\hat{X}(t)\right| \qquad (9.3)$$

MSE – mean square error:

$$MSE = \frac{1}{N}\sum_{t=1}^{N}\left(X(t)-\hat{X}(t)\right)^2 \qquad (9.4)$$

RMSE – root mean square error:

$$RMSE = \sqrt{MSE} \qquad (9.5)$$

ME – mean error:

$$ME = \frac{1}{N}\sum_{t=1}^{N}\left(X(t)-\hat{X}(t)\right) \qquad (9.6)$$

SD – standard deviation:

$$SD = \sqrt{\frac{1}{N}\sum_{t=1}^{N}\left(\hat{X}(t)-ME\right)^2}. \qquad (9.7)$$

Forecast accuracy is an opposite concept to the prediction error. If the forecast error is large, then the accuracy is small and, conversely, if the prediction error is small, then the accuracy is large (Khair et al., 2017). In fact, the forecast error estimate is the inverse of the forecast accuracy – the dependence is simple here:

Forecast accuracy in% = 100% − MAPE (9.8)

Usually, the accuracy is not estimated, in other words, solving the task of forecasting is always evaluated, that is, determine the value of the prediction error, that is, the magnitude and the forecast error. However, it should be understood that if so, then the prediction accuracy = 95%. When talking about high accuracy, we always talk about low forecast error, and there should be no misunderstanding in this area.

In this case, the MAPE is a quantitative estimate of the error itself, and this value clearly tells us the accuracy of prediction, based on the above simple formula. Thus, when estimating the error, we always estimate the accuracy of the prediction.

According to Table 9.2, the best model is a neural network with a nonlinear autoregressive model. You can see the results for the forecast related to Figure 9.6.

Table 9.2 Comparison of Different Methods for the Colds Forecasts

METHOD	MAPE	MAE	MSE	RMSE	ME	SD
Autoregressive model of variable mean	7.1849	29.3399	2069.1879	45.48832	0.1427	45.532
Autoregressive model of variable mean (custom)	6.8860	28.6838	1930.2694	43.9348	0.5027	43.9747
Model of simple exponential smoothing	8.9315	39.2918	4190.0204	64.7303	−0.2436	64.7929
Holt exponential smoothing model	7.9362	35.6543	3899.7392	62.4478	−0.3903	62.5075
Holt-Winters exponential smoothing model	17.5070	75.3171	15462.2587	124.34	−0.9435	57.8242
Neural network with nonlinear autoregressive model	**5.5145**	22.4491	1135.5233	33.6975	−0.043	34.0067
Multilayer perceptron with five hidden layers	6.0216	24.7753	1425.9549	37.7618	−0.1517	37.2962
Multilayer perceptron with automatic detection of the number of hidden layers	6.8004	28.7822	2142.1202	46.2830	0.00071	46.3384
Machine of extreme training	7.3069	31.6591	2605.2752	51.0418	0.0116	51.7630

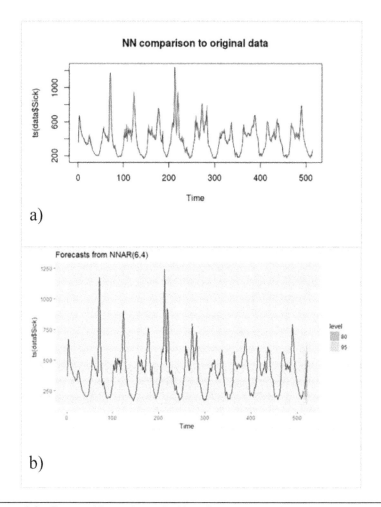

Figure 9.6   Forecast with neural network with nonlinear autoregressive model.

9.6 Implementation of the Data Analytics Methods for the Football Matches Forecasts

For the football matches forecasts let us consider following methods (Harville, 2003):

- Classical Poisson method (Maher, 1982).
- Dickson-Coles method (Dixon and Coles, 1997).
- The method of time-independent least squares Ratings.
- "Predicting football results using a neural network based on FIFA Rating" method (Graham, 2018).

Table 9.3 Comparison of Different Methods for the Football Matches Forecasts

METHOD	MAPE	MAE	MSE	RMSE	ME	SD
Basic Poisson model	9.93	42.03	4479.00	66.9253	0.2373	67.8978
Dixon-Coles method	7.94	35.67	3900.74	62.4559	0.2451	63.1456
Mean square method	7.80	34.68	2783.43	52.7582	0.2092	52.9896
Deep neural network	**6.51**	27.55	2050.45	45.2819	0.1812	45.5678

According to Table 9.3, the best model is the neural network of deep learning (the lowest error rate is 6.51).

9.7　Web-Oriented Tools for Data Analytics

The amount of open data is increasing and it could be effectively used in different fields of studies.

There are numerous web-oriented services which allow user to visualize open data such as world bank open data (https://data. worldbank.org/), Google Public Data Explorer (https://www. google.com/publicdata/directory), Global Health Observatory (https://www.who.int/gho/en/), Registry of Open Data (RODA) on AWS (https://registry.opendata.aws/), They contain open data as already graphical visualization of the data. But it could be more efficient to have a tool which could allow flexibly to manipulate with open data.

An online service was developed by integrating the following frameworks: Laravel (back-end), Vue.js (front-end), Bootstrap, Pyodide, Highcharts, CodeMirror.

The developed service has the following functions (Figure 9.7):

- Creation of the Python scripts.
- Execution of Python scripts.
- Authorization on the server to implement saving scripts in user account.
- CRUD operations on Python scripts.
- Data visualization using Python and JavaScript.
- Download files from the web.
- Python library support (matplotlib, pandas, and numpy).
- Service instruction.

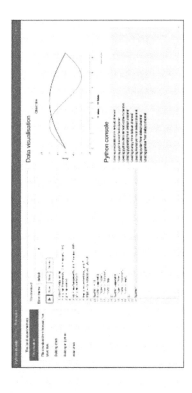

Figure 9.7   Interface of the developed service.

The typical scenario for the usage of the developed service includes the following steps:

- User could select file with data in one of the formats which is acceptable to the open access data requirements (Use Open Standards) – JSON (JavaScript Object Notation); XML/ RDF; TXT/CSV/Markdown.
- User could download .py file with required method or write code directly within the webpage with the usage of the embedded editor.
- Results could be visualized as the graphics and will be printed in the embedded Python console.

9.8 Ethics, Regulations, and Law Constraints for Data Analytics

Analytics and AI are powerful tools that have real-word outcomes. Applying practical, ethical, and legal constructs and scenarios enables getting effective analytics results.

The GDPR, which entered into force last Friday, May 25, guarantees the citizens the ability to decide on the processing of their data through a series of options linked to each of the uses that companies make them or by exercising the rights recognized in the regulations themselves.

Consequently, the new legislation will also limit the use of Big Data that many companies have been developing for commercial or security purposes. It was precisely the concern generated in this area in the European authorities that led to the development of a unifying regulation that would put an end to the gap that the digital revolution has been leaving in recent years.

Therefore, entities must change their strategies in this regard, as the illicit use of customer data could lead them to pay fines of up to 20M EUR in the case of the most serious infractions.

In the search for new solutions that allow them to make legal use of the data generated, risk analysis is the first step that companies will have to take as well as the creation of a figure in charge of making good use of the data of customers. To guarantee this, the companies' control bodies themselves must have sufficient human and material resources to determine whether there is illicit benefit or not in that use of data.

In short, with the application of the GDPR, customers gain power and control over their data, while companies must comply with a series of obligations that limit them in their commercial activities through that data. However, the proper management of this information can be a great opportunity for them because it will lead to more direct and personalized advertising that goes beyond the current analysis and segmentation of customers.

The application of the GDPR, which really came into effect on May 25, 2016, was suspended until this year for companies to have enough time to adapt their regulations in accordance with the new legislation. However, according to a study by Leet Security, 88% of companies have not completed the process of adaptation to the regulations.

9.9 Conclusion

This investigation was aimed at reviewing some relevant data analytics techniques which have been applied to three different case of study: prediction of sports competition results based on open data, the prediction of the cold sickness, and companies' cyber risk assessments.

We have demonstrated that the use of appropriate analysis tools can provide relevant information for the final purpose of each case study. Different parameters have been obtained to assess the quality of the model and the prediction obtained.

The conclusion is that there is no unique method, model, or approach which provides the best results in every scenario. An appropriate study must be performed on the different parameters; in some cases, a preprocessing of the data is required, and the election of the most appropriate regression or classification methods is not trivial.

References

Angierski, A., Kuehn, V. (2013). *Aliasing-tolerant sub-Nyquist sampling of FRI signals*. IEEE International Conference on Communications (ICC). Budapest, pp. 4957–4961. Doi: 10.1109/ICC.2013.6655364.

Bartolini D.N., Benavente-Peces, C., Ahrens, A. (2017a). *Using risk assessments to assess insurability in the context of cyber insurance*. 14th International Joint Conference on e-Business and Telecommunications. (ICETE 2017). Madrid: July 24-26, pp. 337–345.

Bartolini, D.N., Benavente-Peces, C., Ahrens, A. (2017b). *Risk assessment and verification of insurability.* Proceedings of the 7th International Joint Conference on Pervasive and Embedded Computing and Communication Systems. (PECCS 2017). Madrid: July 24-26, pp. 105–108.

Bartolini, D.N., Zascerinska, J., Ahrens, A. (2018a). Instrument design for cyber risk assessment in insurability verification. *Informatics, Control, Measurement in Economy and Environment Protection*, 3, pp. 7–10. Doi. org/10.5604/01.3001.0012.5274.

Bartolini, D.N., Benavente-Peces, C., Ahrens, A. (2018b). *Cyber risk assessment for insurability verification.* Proceedings of the 8th International Joint Conference on Pervasive and Embedded Computing and Communication Systems. (PECCS 2018). Porto: July 29-30, pp. 231–235.

Biener, Ch., Eling, M., Wirfs, J.H. (2015). Insurability of cyber risk: An empirical analysis. *Working Papers on Risk Management and Insurance*, No. 151, January.

Boser, B.E., Guyon, I.M., Vapnik, V.N. (1992). *A training algorithm for optimal margin classifiers.* Proceedings of the 5th Annual Workshop on Computational Learning Theory. COLT '92. New York: ACM, pp. 144–152.

Cortes, C., Vapnik, V. (1995). Support-vector networks. *Machine Learning*, *20(3)*, pp. 273–297.

Dixon, M.J, Coles, S.G. (1997). Modelling association football scores and inefficiencies in the football betting market. *Journal of the Royal Statistical Society: Series C, 46(2)*, pp. 265–280.

Elgendy N., Elragal A. (2014). Big data analytics: A literature review paper. In: P. Perner, (eds.), *Advances in data mining. Applications and theoretical aspects. ICDM 2014. Lecture notes in computer science*, 8557, Cham: Springer, pp. 214–227.

Emmanuel, I., Stanier, C. (2016). *Defining Big Data.* Proceedings of the International Conference on Big Data and Advanced Wireless Technologies. BDAW'16. New York: ACM, pp. 5:1–5:6. Doi:10.1145/3010089.3010090.

Graham, B. (2018). *Predicting football matches using EA player ratings and tensorflow.* Retrieved from: https://towardsdatascience.com/predicting-premier-league-odds-from-ea-player-bfdb52597392. (Access: 10.2019)

Harville, D. (2003). The selection or seeding of college basketball or football teams for postseason competition. *Journal of the American Statistical Association, 98(461)*, pp. 17–27. Retrieved from: http://www.jstor.org/stable/30045190. (Access: 10.2019)

Hyndman, R.J., Athanasopoulos, G. (2018). *Forecasting: Principles and practice, 2nd ed.* Melbourne, Australia: Otexts.

Hyndman, R.J., Koehler, A.B. (2006). Another look at measures of forecast accuracy. *International Journal of Forecasting, 22(4)*, pp. 679–688.

Khair, U., Fahmi, H., Al Hakim S., Rahim, R. (2017). Forecasting error calculation with mean absolute deviation and mean absolute percentage error. *Journal of Physics: Conference Series, 930(1)*.

Maher, M.J. (1982). Modelling association football scores. *Statistica Neerlandica*, *36(3)*, pp. 101–163.

Pyne, S., Rao, P.B.L.S., Rao, S.B. (2016). *Big data analytics: Methods and applications*. New Delhi: Springer. Doi.org/10.1007/978-81-322-3628-3.

Srinivasa, S., Mehta, S. (2014). Big Data analytics. *Third International Conference. BDA 2014*. New Delhi: December 20-23.

Use Open Standards, Open Data, Open Source, and Open Innovation. Retrieved from: https://digitalprinciples.org/principle/use-open-standards-open-data-open-source-and-open-innovation/. (Access: 10.2019).

Index